Mary Barber

The true Narrative of the five years' Suffering & perilous

Adventures

Mary Barber

The true Narrative of the five years' Suffering & perilous Adventures

ISBN/EAN: 9783337180201

Printed in Europe, USA, Canada, Australia, Japan

Cover: Foto ©ninafisch / pixelio.de

More available books at **www.hansebooks.com**

THE TRUE NARRATIVE

OF THE

FIVE YEARS' SUFFERING & PERILOUS ADVENTURES,

BY

Miss Barber,

WIFE OF "SQUATTING BEAR,"

A CELEBRATED SIOUX CHIEF.

MISS BARBER, a native of Massachusetts, in her religious enthusiasm, resolved to go

AMONG THE INDIANS,

as missionary, and with that purpose in view married **Squatting Bear,** at Washington, D. C.

After **five years** of suffering and stirring adventures, this beautiful young lady has just returned East, and her narrative is one of deep and entrancing interest.

A valuable feature of this work is the INDIAN RECEIPTS, given by Miss Barber, for the cure of various diseases. They are very efficacious.

NUMEROUS ACCURATE ENGRAVINGS.

PHILADELPHIA:
BARCLAY & CO., PUBLISHERS
No. 21 NORTH SEVENTH STREET.

MISS BARBER'S NARRATIVE.

CHAPTER I.

MARRIED TO "SQUATTING BEAR."

AM a native of Massachusetts, and was born in June, 1848. Early in life I had those religious principles instilled in my mind which in after years went a great way toward the fixed purpose of becoming an Indian missionary. It has been argued by a great many people—since my return from my five years' sojourn among the Indians—that sentimentalism rather than religious fervor caused the step, which I have since repented, that of marrying an Indian chief.

Kind reader, if there did exist within me a romantic feeling I failed to remark it at the time, nor have I yet detected its existence. I was indeed foolish to have undertaken such a step, but then, in my ignorance, I thought of a great and good work which, by self-sacrifice and resolution, would admit of my success in its accomplishment. I have "lived and learned," and when I turn my thoughts to those eventful years in my life—each one photographed upon my memory, and if further testimony were needed nearly all are recorded in the diary which I kept—I cannot but stand in amazement at perils passed through, and thank the great God above us that I am spared to tell my story, which I claim is one of astonishing adventures such as probably no woman, and few men, have ever experienced.

19

I regret to say that my marriage at Washington, D. C., in 1867, to "Squatting Bear," was by hungry sensation-seekers made the occasion of a public demonstration, against my wish. But there is no need to review that portion of my life; you are all familiar with its every detail, the press throughout this country and Europe having freely vented the particulars.

"Squatting Bear," my husband, is a chief of the Sioux Indian Tribe which is divided into several families, his family being called "Brule." All male Indians are named according to some incident occurring during their early life. If the incident be one of a bur-lesque or cowardly nature the name thus derived may be afterwards changed by some act of bravery. But where the name is in the first place gained by a brave act it is never altered. To illustrate— my husband's brother, when about twenty years of age, started with two of his tribe on a hunt. On their way they came to a river with a very rapid current, requiring in a man considerable strength to swim it. His companions were ahead and gained the shore before him; turning they saw him hold up one hand, and heard him cry "cowaree" (cramp). They rescued him, and on their return to the Indian village gave him the name, which they had heard the traders use, and had a slight idea of its definition—"Belly-ache," which he retained for many years; having fortunately afterward, however, gained celebrity for keenness of vision, he was re-named — "Keen-eye."

The way my husband gained his somewhat unromantic appella-tion was through the following incident. In company with a "brave" he one day started out with the avowed intention of killing a "waunoe" (bear) which had, for several days, been seen wandering in the neighborhood of the encampment. They walked many miles without discovering any signs of the animal, when suddenly the bear sprang upon my husband, and so quick was the encounter that both man and beast in the sudden contact were thrown upon their backs. My husband, then known as Temulle, endeavored to regain his feet, but the bear seemed in no way disposed to allow such an

action, for she immediately "closed in" and hugged Temulle to her
heart's content. This affectionate reception in no manner pleased
the Indian. His companion "Tall-oak" did not dare to fire, and
during the struggle Temulle called to him forbidding him to, in any
way, interfere with him, as he wished to fight it out alone.

The struggle was long and fierce, and not once did Temulle find
himself able to get upon his feet. Over and over rolled man and
beast. Temulle was by this time terribly gashed and bled profusely.
Now he would manage to get upon his knees, and with all his
strength, which was great, succeed in hurling his antagonist from
him. But to no effect, for before he could regain his feet the bear
was upon him. The witness to this encounter thinking every new
and then that Temulle was overcome would say, " 'Tall-oak,' now
help Temulle," to which he would reply, "Not so, Temulle fights
his own battles, to Temulle belongs the victory." After a prolonged
fight the bear was killed. Temulle's knife had entered the bear's
heart. This incident gave to Temulle the name of "Squatting
Bear."

But I digress. The world knows of my marriage to, and departure with, Squatting Bear. We went from Washington to Chicago,
from there to Des Moines, Iowa; thence to Omaha, Nebraska, where
we remained several days for the purpose of making purchases.
Along the route we were greeted either with cheers, or shouts of
derision, from the crowds assembled at the different railroad depots.
Many enthusiastic church people having heard of my mission were
awaiting, in the cities along our route, my arrival. Some offered
me money, others had dainties put up in jars and baskets, but the
greater portion insisted upon my taking bibles, hymn books, etc.
A few of these, in my zeal, I accepted, little thinking how useless
they were where I was going. Thinking! Why, bless you, I never
stopped to think at all, for if I had I should never have taken the
step I did, and consequently these lines would never have seen print.

There was I going among a people, the greater portion of
whom could not understand me, for the purpose of converting

them to Christianity, and leaving behind a more promising field of
heathens. During our journey my husband was very kind
to me—the sort of kindness a child displays toward a toy: but
I paid but little attention to him then, for my mind was religiously
pre-occupied.

Did I love him? per haps some may ask. No, I did not; and
that one thought has since given me much uneasiness. 'Twas a sin
to marry a man whom I did *not* love. But, reader, I pray your
lenience. Remember I was young and blind with what I then considered a religious duty. I have read articles since my return (1872)
in several papers, and among them a Journal of the Church, con-
demning me severely—asserting that it was " nothing but the romance
and folly in the head of a silly girl which induced her to wed herself with an Indian, *pretending*, or *imagining* that it was in the cause
of religion." This I positively deny, for however foolish the step—
and that I acknowledge—it was in the cause of religion, and for that
only, that I did it. But no more of this ; I did not commence this
narrative for the purpose of self-justification, and shall tire my readers
with no such pleadings ; so follow me without fear. As I have said,
we spent a few days in Omaha.

One day my husband came to me with the information that we
were to start the following morning at sunrise, and ordered me to
make preparations accordingly. So we started, and in due
time reached Sioux City, where we remained but a short time, and
then struck up the Yankton river. At length we arrived at Yankton, Dakota, and then the real journey commenced. The "Brules"
village lay to the right about one hundred and forty-three miles
from Yankton. We were provided with horses, which we had pur-
chased at Sioux City We had accomplished some forty-five miles
the first day when my husband concluded to rest. I was thoroughly
tired out, and no such luxury as a bed awaited me, but I had anticipated such hardships and bravely lay me down to sleep. I had no
difficulty in doing this, for nature soon asserted her control, and
refreshing sleep claimed possession of my exhausted energies. In the

MARRIAGE TO "SQUATTING BEAR," THE INDIAN CHIEF, AT WASHINGTON, D. C.

Seine Verheirathung mit „Hockebär" dem indianischen Häuptling, zu Washington, D. C.

morning I awoke somewhat *stiff*, but *hopeful*, and it occurred to me that I should first make a convert of my Indian husband. Alas! my first attempt was enough to discourage any one. "Woman talk to woman, no tell *man* what he must do." That was the end of that attempt at conversion.

I subsequently learned, what had before been a strong doubt in my mind, that the *noble* Indian has nothing but ignoble wives, or that the "squaw" is forced in most cases, to do all the menial labor, is in fact a slave. This is not always the case, but to find an Indian allowing his wife to suit her own inclinations is indeed a rarity. Some Indians have several "squaws," and among them one favorite who is allowed more privileges than the others. And yet I have found (not in my own case, but by observing other cases) Indian courtship to be of the most romantic description—indeed romance forms the greater part of the Indian nature. but like many of their "*white* brethren," the lover dies in giving birth to the husband.

I have seen and cruelly felt the usage accorded the squaw. Most Indians look upon their wives or squaws as beasts of burden. It is among the commonest sights in the Indian, even among the partly "civilized" aborigines, to see a sturdy fellow mounted on his pony, with a gun across the saddle as his only burden, while his wife or wives follow in his trail, with the whole furniture of the "lodge" lashed upon her, or their backs, and, in addition to this, leading a horse or cow by the halter—he riding along with the air of a king, and she trudging over the ground like a "pack-mule," lucky if she escapes kicks and blows.

How I digress again, to be sure; but I can't help it, I have so much to relate that I scarcely know how to commence. Our second night's halt was on the stream of a beautiful roaring brook, called by the Indians "Naog," which signifies *roaring*. Never shall I forget the scene which took place on that stream that night. The moon shone brightly, and not a sound, except the falling water, disturbed my meditation. I should judge that it was about ten o'clock when we were both startled by the sound of horses' feet, my husband ever on the alert stood upon his guard. The horse soon dashed by us, disclosing an Indian rider. Temulle (I like that name better than "Squatting-Bear") hailed him; he reined up, and seemed in doubt as to the advisability of returning. My husband advanced and pointed his gun at him, at the same time ordering him to advance and dismount which he did. The following coversation, in the Brule tongue, which my husband repeated in English, ensued:

"Whence come ye?"

"From the Blackfeet nation."

"You are a nord-Sioux."

"Yes, my brother speaks truly

(Here a long silence ensued, which was broken by Temulle, who during this time had eyed the other Indian in a manner which set him ill at ease.)

"There has been blood between the Sioux and Blackfeet?"

"Yes."

"Why did you leave?"

'We were in battle with our enemies against great numbers. The dead lay around us counting many. The Great Spirit forsook us."

"And you fled?"

"Yes" (hanging his head down).

"Your name?"

"Manamoor."

"Go thou to the Great Spirit and tell him I, Temulle, have sent him a coward that he may know thee as thou art."

As Temulle said these words he drew a pistol—which had been presented to him at Washington—and shot Manamoor to the heart. He then took the lifeless body and tied it to a tree; this done, he took his scalping-knife and drew two peculiar marks across the forehead, which he informed me signified that the dead Indian had lived a coward. This was the first of a series of horrible sights which I was afterwards doomed to behold, and the reader may perhaps imagine the dreadful effect it produced upon my nerves, which were

.n no manner strengthened by the words shortly after spoken by
my husband :

"Squaw, prepare to move; my tribe is at war, Temulle goes to
meet his enemies, Blackfeet die by hundreds. Come!"

So I was forced to continue my journey, and at last completely
worn out I, in company with Temulle, reached the Brule village.
This Indian village did not differ, in point of appearance, from most
of those I have since seen. And I will here take occasion to con-
clude one chapter and commence another, which will give my readers
some idea of the Indian physically and morally, their religion and
superstitions being duly considered.

CHAPTER II.

THE Indians generally are disposed to rove; and in their excursions they frequently encroach on the privileges of their neighbors, which is seldom suffered to pass unnoticed and usually terminates in war: a result frequently courted with no other view than to school the young warriors, and afford the older ones opportunities to acquire distinction. These wars are sometimes of short duration; at others they only cease with the extermination, or removal of one of the parties.

When a nation of Indians becomes too numerous conveniently to procure subsistence from its own hunting-grounds, it is no uncommon occurrence for it to send out a colony, or in other words, to separate into tribes, or families. Thus with the Sioux there are the Brulé, (my husband's tribe), the Nordos, Washaukee, Wannie, etc. Preparatory to such a measure, runners or spies are sent in various directions to ascertain the most suitable location. A national council next hears the several reports, determines on the plan, and elects chiefs to carry it into operation. The pipe is then sent round, and all who smoke it are considered volunteers. When the number is properly proportioned the ceremony of separation takes place, is at once accomplished, and is truly affecting. The tribe so separated maintains all its relations, independent of the parent nation, though the most friendly intercourse is commonly maintained, and they are almost uniformly allies. Separations sometimes take place from party dissensions, growing generally out of the jealousies of the principal chiefs, and not unfrequently out of petty quarrels These divisions seldom last long, reconciliation follows reflection and a re-union is effected. Instances, however, I have known, in which the two parties become the most irreconcilable, rancorous, and deadly foes, and raised the tomahawk against each other, with a malignity surpassing, if possible, that exercised between hostile nations totally distinct in consanguinity.

It has been supposed by some, that all the Indian nations speak different dialects of the same language, but the case is far otherwise. There are scarcely two nations between whom no intercourse exists, whose languages are so similar, as to be mutually understood by the respective individuals of each; indeed, I fully believe there are none, although the circumstance of origin, descent, immediate neighborhood, intermarriages, voluntary associations, friendly intercourse, and the incorporation of the vanquished of one tribe with another, have materially modified, and, in many instances, effected a strong resemblance in some of them.

Among nations more remote, some words of the same pronunciation, and of the same and different imports, are used; but instances of this nature do not occur sufficiently often to materially alter their character, and they maintain their distinctiveness, with as much force perhaps as do the English, French, German, and Russian languages. It is true that an individual of one nation may, by the assistance of signs, make himself sufficiently understood to hold a conversation on all ordinary subjects, with strangers of almost every other; but then it should be remembered, that their languages partake greatly of the pantomimic, and that their poverty is, to a considerable degree, made up for by those impressive and common auxiliaries. The Indian languages suffer frequent and considerable changes.

In regard to the signs used by Indians to connect their words or render their languages intelligible, very little of a satisfactory nature can be said; because they are so variously adapted to their different subjects of conversation as in general to baffle description. In order to comprehend them fully it is necessary to understand their idioms and habits.

In talking of an enemy they assume a ferocious attitude and aspect, seize hold of, and brandish their weapons of war, in precisely the same manner as they would do if they were in his presence, and about to engage in a deadly conflict. The wampum and pipe are handled in conversations on peaceful subjects, and everything con- nected with them is diametrically reversed.

In speaking of men, game, birds, trees, marching, hunting, swim ming, etc., etc., the Indian displays a wonderful power for acting and imitating, and the peculiarity of each, individually, is imitated in so happy a manner, as to be readily understood by those ac- quainted with the qualities of the subject intended to be described, although they should be entire strangers to the language.

In their writing and correspondence, the Indians make use alto- gether of hieroglyphics. It is doubtful if they had a knowledge of methodical combination whether their language would admit of its use. They inscribe their correspondence, and such subjects as require to be recorded, on the inner bark of the white birch, or on skins prepared for the purpose. In the reasoning, the judgment and perceptions of an Indian are, generally speaking, clear and quick, and their arguments ingenious and cogent.

In respect to the origin of their religion, the Indians themselves are altogether ignorant. It is certain, however, that they acknowl- edge, at least so far as my acquaintance extends, one supreme, all powerful, and intelligent Being, viz.: the "Great Spirit," or the Giver of Life, who created and governs all things.

They believe, in general, that after the hunting grounds had been formed and supplied with game, that he created the first red man and woman, who were very large in their stature, and lived to an exceedingly old age; that he often held councils with them, gave them laws to be observed, and taught them how to take game and cultivate corn, but that in consequence of their disobedience, he withdrew from, and abandoned them to the Wallertozcor, (Bad Spirit,) who had since been instrumental to all their degeneracy and sufferings. [This fact singularly coincides, in a great measure, with

MY DOMESTIC DUTIES PRACTISED UNDER DIFFICULTY. JEALOUSY OF
ME-EM-O-LE.

Meine häuslichen Pflichten unter Schwierigkeit ausgeübt. Eifersucht von Me-em-o-le.

our Bible view of earth's formation, and the story of Adam and Eve in the "Happy Land of Paradise," and will afford a subject for meditation, when we consider that the story has been familiar to the Indians before the white man came among them.] They believe the Great Spirit to be of a too exalted character to be directly the author of evil, and that, notwithstanding the offences of his red children, he continues to shower down on them all the bless'ngs they enjoy'; in consequence of this parental regard for them, they are truly filial and sincere in their devotions to him for such things as they need, and return thanks for such good things as they receive.

On the other hand, when in affliction, or suffering under any great calamity, in the belief that it will appease his wrath or miti gate his chastisements, they pray with equal fervency to the Evil Spirit, who, they conceive, is a character directly the reverse of the Good Spirit, to whom he is inferior, but, nevertheless, has sufficient power, and is constantly devising means to torment and punish them. By the term spirit, the Indians have an idea of a being that can, at pleasure, be present, and yet invisible; they nevertheless think the Great Spirit, like themselves, possessed of a corporeal form, though endowed with a nature infinitely more excellent than theirs, and which will endure forever without change. Although they believe in a future state of existence, they associate it with natural things. Their "hunting ground" or heaven, they believe, will be a place where game is abundant, and where there is perpetual spring and cloudless sky.

They expect that their sensual pleasures will be in proportion to individual merit; the brave warrior, expert hunter, and those slain in battle in defence of their country, having the highest claims, will be the most distinguished; while those of subordinate pretensions, will occupy subordinate positions.

They have no particular days set apart for devotional purposes, though they have particular times; such, for instance, as declaration of war, the restoration of peace, and extraordinary natural visitations. Their manner of worshipping the Deity differs on

different occasions. Shortly after a council of war, every individual
that is able to walk, and the old men sometimes borne by others,
assemble in a grove, or some other place rendered sacred by the
occasion, and offer up their prayers to the Great Spirit for success
against their enemies.

Sometimes the devotional exercises are pantomimic and profoundl
silent; at others, ejaculatory and vociferous. As I progress with
my narrative I shall take occasion to remark upon other customs
of the Indians and their costumes, etc., but I must now take up the
actual thread of my story.

CHAPTER III.

WHEN we arrived at the Brule village I witnessed for the first time Indians at devotional exercises. Our arrival amongst them did not cause the slightest interruption to their ceremony (an example which might well be imitated by their white brethren). At the conclusion we learned that the difficulty which Manamoor had related as having occurred with the Blackfeet had been amicably adjusted. The Indians gathered around us, and after their manner welcomed Temulle's white squaw. In that moment I imagined everything. I thought I saw looks of jealousy and hatred dart forth from the eyes of my dusky sex thereat assembled—at one moment I expected to see them rush upon me and tear me to pieces. At length some of the Indian maidens came directly up to me and examined my costume critically. The male portion of the village then withdrew, and Temulle, who had been to see the Great Chief at Washington (Johnson), was, for the time being, the hero.

Meanwhile I was an object of the greatest curiosity to the red-skin females. Many of them could speak a little English, but there were but two with whom I could converse with any satisfaction. One of these I had noticed standing aloof from the others, and although she looked towards me, there was not that amount of brazenness in her glance which could be plainly seen in the eyes and manners of the others. I beckoned to her, and she came grace-fully to me. She was of rare beauty, compared with her companions, and in her eyes, which were blue, there dwelt a world of soul

"What is your name?" I asked.

"Deitosie." (The meaning of which is "from the Great Spirit.")

'That is a very pretty name, and you are a very pretty girl."

"Does my sister think I know not that? Each stream of water tells me one, and the sound of the other is sufficient."

"Will Deitosie walk with me toward my chief's hut?"

She consented, and arm in arm we walked toward the centre of the village, where, pointing out a hut, decorated with blankets and buffalo robes, many of which were gorgeously painted, she informed me that there I could rest. Accordingly, after taking a general survey of the interior, I lay me down and soon fell asleep. When I awoke Deitosie stood beside me, and my first glance met her eyes. She smiled sweetly, and I arose from my couch.

She inquired if I slept well, and on my answering in the affirma-tive, she proposed a walk, to which I freely consented. Just as we were about to leave the hut, there entered an old squaw and a young one about fourteen years of age, I should judge. With mercy a glance at them. taking it for granted that one was the mother, and the other the sister of Temulle, I followed Deitosie. We had walked some distance, when my companion turned and asked me to relate her my history. I did so, and gradually turned our conversation upon religion. We conversed for some time, and I may as well here state that Deitosie became a devout convert, as did also one other Indian maiden, of whom I shall have occasion to hereafter speak.

We had walked a long way from the village, when we came to a beautiful mountain path. Up this we went until the summit was reached. Here we sat down near the edge of a frightful abyss. Deitosie related a legend connected with this particular spot.

Many years ago an Indian maiden who had married a 'Brave," and by him given birth to a child, was in the habit of visiting the spot to meet the return of her husband. In the same tribe there was another brave who had been, before her marriage, very per-sistent in his attentions toward her. She did not love Wannotee.

which was the name of her rejected lover, and so gave her heart to Sumsumot. One evening she repaired to the meeting place as usual with her child in her arms. She had been there but a short time, when Wannotee was seen by her coming up the path. There was nothing strange in this, so she paid no attention to his approach. In an instant he was by her side, and pouring into her ears such proposals as no squaw who loves her brave would listen to. With flashing eyes she sprang to her feet and demanded his instant departure. He merely laughed scornfully, and springing toward her he seized her in his arms. She struggled bravely, but to no purpose, as she was but a child in the iron hands of Wannotee. With a piercing scream, she cried for help. The voice of Sumsumot was heard in response, and ere long he dashed in sight, on the rock directly above them. Sumsumot, in a clear ringing voice, commanded his rival to unhand his wife under pain of instant death. For answer Wannotee shouted, " Fire but one shot, and your squaw and papoose I su_" hurl below me."

During this time the Indian wife was making fearful struggles to release herself, and Wannotee was being backed, without knowing it, toward the brink of the frightful abyss. The despair of Sumsumot who witnessed this scene was terrible. To leave his position on the rock and reach his wife in time to save her from being thrown into the abyss was impossible. To fire was a great risk as he might shoot his wife or child. He then opened a parley with his fiendish opponent. Wannotee would agree but to one thing— Sumsumot must swear by the Great Spirit to give him his squaw, and take his papoose where he chose. In the agony of despair, at hearing these words, Sumsumot fired upon Wannotee, the shot took effect, and for a moment he relinquished his hold upon the woman, who, terrified beyond description, stood perfectly still, nor made no effort to escape. Wannotee staggered and seemed about to drop dead, when with one last, almost superhuman effort, he sprang towards the Indian woman, seized her in his arms, and with a wonderful leap cleared the edge of the abyss. The shout of Wannotee and the chilling scream of the woman greeted Sumsumot, a crashing sound followed, and then all was still as death.

Sumsumot, for a time, lay senseless, but recovering himself he arose with the face of a demon. His Indian nature panted for revenge; he went back to the village, related his story to four chiefs, and then, with knife and gun, killed all of Wannotee's relatives. He then ran, followed by the braves of the village, who were so astounded at the murders, and the rapidity with which he committed them, that they were powerless for the time to restrain him. Sum-sumot ran until he arrived at the abyss where the tragedy occurred, and with a look and cry of despair, leaped into the darkness below. The remains were afterwards found by some Indians, who erected a rude monument on the spot, and ever afterwards the rock upon which Deitosie and I sat, was known as "Cantowinnie" (Abyss of Despair).

Afterward, in conversation with Deitosie, I learned, with feelings of disgust and surprise, that the little Indian girl, and the old squaw whom I had seen entering Temulle's hut, were his wives. The girl could not have been fourteen years of age—in fact was *not*, as I afterward learned—and the old squaw was nearly sixty. Certainly this information was enough to upset all feelings of romance, had I ever entertained any; but it was not that which hurt me so, it was the idea of being wedded to a man who already had two other wives.

Deitosie and myself soon arrived at the village, and there I was formally introduced by my husband to his wives, Nos. 1 and 2; and afterwards the chiefs came in one at a time and spoke some oily language relative to their feelings of respect and admiration for their "white daughter."

The next day found me awake bright and early, but not before Temulle, who had been up an hour sooner. As I made my exit from the door of the hut I met him. He saluted me, half in the manner of a cavalier, and that of a person who had gained a victory, and beheld his captive. I asked him what were to be my duties, and expressed a willingness to commence at once. He answered me thus:—

THE INDIAN WAR DANCE. — Der indianische Kriegs-Tanz.

"White squaw do to look at sometime; when me want her work, me tell her so. Let the other tw. work for you."

I may here remark, that my husband's English was not so pure as that of Deitosie. The latter, by the way, was of the Cheyenne tribe. Her father had been one of a body of Indians who split from the main body because of a quarrel, and being driven from one spot to another, himself, daughter, and a young Cheyenne brave, Lissassa by name, had joined the Brule-Sioux.

During my second day I conversed religiously with all the Indians willing to listen, who could understand English. My first attempt was anything but encouraging, and I finally concluded to give it up until I could master the Sioux language. This I did, I may say, easily, and before long I was enabled to offer up prayers to Him who was, I taught them, the Great Spirit of all men, women, and children, no matter what their color might be. My attempts to teach and reform the Indian children were treated with indifference and contempt, and I may perhaps be allowed some credit, when I assert that I continued under the discouraging auspices nearly one year, and during that time made two converts—Deitosie and Winnotestee, (my husband's young wife).

I had been among the Sioux about six months, when an event occurred, which horrified me extremely. One day a number of braves returned from a hunting expedition, accompanied by a soldier of the U. S. Army, en costume, whom they had captured. The braves reported that he had deserted from his company, and had for some time past been amusing himself by lying in ambuscade and shooting Indians as they passed. In conversation with him shortly after his arrival, he informed me that he had received his discharge, (which he showed me,) and had started home in company with a party of hunters, from whom he became lost. He belonged to the thirty-second U. S. Infantry; but I have forgotten his name. The Indians had, without doubt, confounded him with another man whom he had heard of, and whose name was Fly Jones, but he had gained from the Indians the appellation of "Indiamo Apes" (Indian killer).

My sympathies were, of course, aroused in this poor man's behalf. But what could I do? And yet, perhaps, my husband might exert his influence for my sake. I concluded to ask him. Temulle's jealousy was greatly aroused, when I appeared before him and upon my knees besought him to plead for the soldier's life. He accused me of wishing the "pale face" to become my lover; and this attempt at the "Pocahontas business" ended by my being placed in the hut under guard of the old hag, and the little child-wife.

During the day of the capture the old hags and boys of the village were permitted to torment the prisoner with taunts, shooting headless arrows at him, sticking him with Indian toy-knives, etc. At night the stake, at which he was to be burned, was driven in the ground; and soon after the soldier was brought forward, bound securely, and dry brush heaped around him. Temulle, in a jealous fit, desired that I should witness the scene. I protested, but to no effect, and was forced to go to the spot. I endeavored to close my eyes to this dreadful scene, but could not.

Once tied to the stake the Indians amused themselves for about an hour, by throwing the tomahawk; the object being to see how near they could come to hitting his head— without touching it. None but experts were allowed to participate in this amusement, and their dexterity was truly astonishing. With closed eyes the prisoner stood, and awaited his death, for he evidently did not know but what they were trying, in this manner, to split his head open. This amusement over, the brush was carefully placed around him. Then the Indians drew lots, but for what, I could not at the moment perceive. I was not left long in doubt, for the successful Indian stepped out from the circle, and in a moment had completely scalped the soldier. At this horrible sight I fainted; and when I returned to consciousness, the prisoner's body was burned as far up as his chest, and the crisp flesh was rapidly falling into the fire beneath him. Life by this time was extinct; but there, with the eyes starting from their sockets, was his head, with ghastly appearance, still against the post, his neck having been securely fastened. This second awful sight caused another fainting spell, and just before I lost consciousness this time, I could see the squaws around me, and hear their jeers at the weakness of the sickly pale face squaw.

These horrible scenes so worked upon my nerves, that for two days I lay in a helpless condition. During that time I resolved to escape, if a possibility of such a feat presented itself. The second day of my illness brought with it a visit from Deitosie, who was accompanied by a tall fine looking Indian, whom she informed me, (aside,) was thought to be crazy by the Brule tribe; but who, she assured me, was far from being a lunatic. Trouble had brought upon him eccentric manners.

After conversing awhile with Deitosie, I opened a correspondence with the young Indian chief, who eventually allowed himself to run into his old train of thoughts, and I finally persuaded him to give me his story of sufferings, adventure, and sorrow, in full. of which I propose making a separate chapter.

CHAPTER IV.

MY tribe is that which was once known only as the "Dako-tas," but the greater part of which is now termed the Sioux. My people have wronged me greatly, and I shall never return to them. My people are mostly what you term savages, and many of them are drunkards, the in-fluence of your civilization being forced upon them principally in the shape of "fire-water." To become a chief among the Sioux. one must, at least, have scalped a warrior of another tribe, and prove to have done so, by producing the scalp; I was not naturally dis posed to acquire either of these bloody trophies, and consequently I was despised as a coward by my people; although I had never shown any fear in fighting or exposing my life, whenever we in vaded the territory of the Pawnees, with whom we were constantly in warfare.

During one of these expeditions, I ventured myself rather near one of the Pawnee villages, many miles distant from our country, expecting to find an opportunity for some exploit of bravery or skill; which might prove that I was not such a coward as my peo-ple supposed me to be, for none of them had ever gone alone so near, or rather among the Pawnees, being thus exposed to their scalping knife, and full vent of their hatred.

Seeing no warrior about the village, that the main body of its warriors was absent on an excursion; so I laid myself down in an ambush among the bushes, where I waited for some adventure. The great light of the world had already sunk half its way down, when I saw a beautiful Pawnee girl approaching me, as innocently

44

⇠ a lamb might approach a hidden wolf. I did not stu but let her pass by, while I scarcely breathed for fear I should frighten her. As she passed I withdrew a little from my concealment, and turning she saw me. At first she was startled. I arose to my feet; but instead of running away she stood still, and waited until I had reached her, when she smiled and said: "Although you are a Sioux, vou will neither kill nor strike me; for your eyes look mild, and they speak a language which tells me you are good and brave and would not harm me."

This confiding address disarmed me, and throwing away my weapons to show my friendly intentions, I said in reply, "Fair maiden, your words are sweet, and your features vie with tne brilliancy of the morning sun. If I were not a Sioux, I would be a Pawnee and hunt for you alone. Tell me your name, fair maiden."

She looked down and said: "Although you are a Sioux, I like to believe in your friendliness, and shall. First tell me your name."

"Waanataa!"

"Then you are the grandson of the far-famed chief? Well, my name is Diora, the daughter of Petalso, whom they call the bravest of the braves."

"Then," said I, "Diora, the daughter of Petalso, is a fit companion for Waanataa. Will she accompany him as his squaw?"

She made answer: "Diora is an orphan now. No Pawnee has yet moved her heart. She has seen Waanataa and will follow him."

When she concluded I caught her in my arms, invoking the sanction and aid of the Great Spirit to our union, and answered in delight from my soul: "Diora has my heart, none other shall have my lodge, and for thee alone will I hunt the forest game."

We then sat down and ate together our first common meal, a portion of my provisions taken along with me, looking and smiling at each other. Some hours past until we thought of leaving, a difficulty by no means easily got over, when, as if to aid our flight, the sun became obscured by passing clouds, which were of a settled nature, and would thus hide the moon's rising, and favor our flight toward my home

We lked along swiftly, but in silence, until the bright morning
star a   ded from beyond the far mountains, and joy lighted up its
face; a welcome to us gave. Suddenly I heard a distant noise,
and before long the war whoop of the Pawnee rang in our ears.
Diora trembled, and exclaimed: "Mackatana-Namakee! (Black
Thunder.) His band, they are going to invade your country!" I
tried to soothe my frightened dove who now informed me, in a few
words, that she had some time ago refused to become the squaw of
Black Thunder, the leader of the body of Pawnee now approaching.

I had almost given up in despair, when, to my great surprise and
intense gratification, 1 beheld three horses, caparisoned with Pawnee
saddles, tied to trees directly in front of us. Without stopping to
inquire for their owners, I hastily seated Diora on one, mounted
myself upon another, and with a joyful heart urged them onward.
The swiftness and strength of our noble horses coulu alone save us
from destruction at the hands of Black Thunder, whose vengeance
would thus be doubly satisfactory, on account of rejected love and
of national hatred. But I was resolved that he should neither capture my bride, nor dance round my scalp; and we dashed along at
a wonderful speed, for of noble blood our suddenly acquired horses
proved.

Thus we flew o'er the ground, followed closely by Black Thunder,
who had now obtained a sight of us. On, on, we went, the demon
Pawnee and his band following like a gloomy cloud chased by winds,
whose howling was more than outdone by the dreadful war whoop of
our fierce pursuers. Two of my pursuers were greatly in advance of
the others. When the foremost got near enough, he fired his rifle at
us, but in vain. I then wielded and stopped my horse, aimed and
fired, whereupon my would-be assassin fell from his horse, dead;
but in the meantime the other Pawnee had reached to within aiming
distance, when he too fired upon us, but luckily without effect. He
still pushed forward however, and seeing that we were likely to end
this scene by a hand-to-hand encounter, I dismounted, giving my
horse's rein to Diora, whom I bade hold fast and remain near me,

" MY SUFFERING KNEW NO BOUNDS. THE FIEND WAS AT NO LOSS TO DEVISE
SCHEMES OF TORTURE."

„Meine Leiden nahmen kein Ende. Der Feind kam nie in Verlegenheit, neue Qualen zu erfinden."

I had hardly dismounted, when, with an angry snort my horse je ked loose from her grasp, and ran away. This was unfortunate, but there was no time for thoughts of that kind, for my antagonist was now upon me.

As he came near he cast a glance toward Diora. A sudden furious yell escaped him; but I claimed his attention with my tomahawk, which clanked against his with repeated strokes, till at length e lost his balance, and fell from his horse with a heavy groan, for with a sudden blow, in which was centred all my strength, I brought my tomahawk down with a force which sent it slicing through his right shoulder and completely severed his arm from his body. In falling his foot caught in the stirrup, and his head came in violent contact with a rock close by. He now seemed to wait for being scalped and killed; but I, although his fair vanquisher, declined taking the trophy, nor did I kill him; to save Diora was my only purpose, and I should feel my cheeks with very shame burning, had I struck a conquered and fallen enemy.

With a leap I now swung myself upon the back of Black Thunder's horse, leaving its owner prostrate, and about half dead on the ground; for I had no time to spare, as my enemies were now in a body close upon me. It would have been madness to confront this great number, and wisely I decided in favor of flight.

My enemies, as soon as they came to their fallen leader, stopped, and remained busily engaged about him; while every moment thus spent was a new lease of life to me and mine. He was perhaps induced, by my generosity in sparing his life and in not scalping him, to forbid his warriors all further pursuit of us, or remained unconscious, or was dead; and they would not fight without him, for we saw no more of them that day.

Diora was very talkative, both in riding and resting; and related to me some very interesting incidents of her father's and grandfather's tribes, which I now try to repeat in her own words, as near as possible:—

"Wher my father was still very young, though he had already

4

distinguished himself in battles, for which our people esteemed him
as a chief, the Pawnees made war on the Iteans, of whom a young
squaw was captured by one of our warriors.

"He gave her up to the medicine-man, who doomed her to be
burned alive at the stake, in sacrifice to the Great Star. Leteel, my
great and famous grandfather, whom they called with great respect
the *Knife-chief*, had always opposed that old cruel custom of our
people; but they listened more to the medicine-man, than to him,
except in warfare. So the unfortunate Itean squaw was bound to
the stake around which our people assembled in large crowds, to
see her die in the flames.

"My father was sitting silent among the spectators. The flames
had nearly reached their intended victim, when, lo! the young chief
stood suddenly by her side, tore the binding ropes asunder, and
carried her in his arms past the perplexed crowds, to a place at
some distance, where he had previously fastened two swift horses.
These horses they mounted and soon disappeared from the view of
the astonished multitude. He conveyed her safe to the Itean country; and returned to his own, unconcerned at the consequences of
his daring act, which no other Pawnee warrior would have done;
but none durst censure him, not even the medicine-man, who was
the most disappointed of all; and the virtuous Leteel approved the
good action of his noble son, of whom he was not a little proud.

"Before getting married, my father was sent by our people to
the Great Father at Washington, the big village of the whites,
where their fine and young squaws tried every means to move his
heart, and loved him very much; because they had heard how he
rescued the young Itean squaw, telling him he was brave, good,
everything that was noble, and they gave him a medal made of
metal bright which they called silver, and on it were marks, which
were to mean such fine words, that I learned them by heart from my
mother, who to me repeated them so often: '*Brother*, accept this
token of our esteem; always wear it for our sakes, and when again
you have the power to save a young woman from torture or from

death, remember this and us, and try to her rescue.' He wore that medal attached to a string, and was very proud of it. When he died, he requested to be buried with it still around his neck.

"After his return from the wigwam of the white chief, he went to the Itean village, and brought back with him the maiden whom he had saved; and she was my mother. I am justly proud of my father the 'Bravest of the Braves.'"

(Here Waanataa sighed deeply; and after quite a silence, he proceeded with *his* story.)

It was a fine sunny morning when we reached my native place; one of the villages in the Sioux country, and belonged to the Lo tribe. The appearance of a Pawnee squaw there was so extraordinary an event, that in a few moments after our arrival, we were surrounded by a crowd of men, women, and children. Our Sioux squaws looked first with evident jealousy at my beautiful Diora; however, they could not for a long time resist her charming innocence; and when she entreated them, with tears in her handsome eyes, to adopt her as a sister and daughter, their hearts melted towards her. My fellow-warriors did not, particularly the younger ones, show any marks of opposition when I publicly declared her to be my wife; but eventually, some of the aged warriors, in accordance with, and probably instigated by our old medicine-man, became violently opposed to my union with a Pawnee squaw. They stuck to their old customs, which did not allow intermarriage between Sioux and Pawnees; and the present war between the two tribes was far from favoring an exception in our behalf.

My friendly endeavors to conciliate my old, stubborn opponents failed; and I was too isolated among my companions, on account of my peaceable disposition, and my antipathy to scalping and killing our prisoners, or else I would have made a violent resistance to such cruel oppression. I determined upon the use of cunning to circumvent my oppressors, who had really organized a conspiracy to ruin me; which purported that I myself had conspired against my own people, having as they asserted, become a friend to their enemies, the Pawnees, to whom they said I would betray them whenever I could.

It lay in my plan seemingly to yield and submit, as far as I could, to whatever our people's council should decide concerning my marriage with Diora; but indeed I was resolved rather to die with her than live without her. One day I returned from hunting, and did not find her before our lodge, where she usually waited for my return. Instead of her, I found there an old warrior, who had always been my friend, and who informed me that she was a prisoner in the lodge of our medicine-man; that it was surrounded by a body of our warriors, and that I could not see her until we both should undergo a public examination, to be held the next day before our council. He added that she had refused to answer any question, except in my presence, and with my consent, declaring, " Diora does not fear any of you; for she is the grand-daughter of Leteel, the daughter of Petalso, and the *wife of Waanataa !*"

This unexpected boldness on her part, who had always been so quiet and modest. had greatly astonished and puzzled them all. They had been so awe-struck at hearing those celebrated names in such a connection with hers and mine, that none spoke a word in reply to her, whose origin had been a secret to every one of them ; but my mind misgave me bad consequences, from exposing that secret in the present circumstances. Unable now to do anything for her rescue—for what could I do but die in fighting alone?—I suffered and waited with great impatience the dawn of the coming day, when all the warriors of our village assembled before the lodge of our medicine-man, who presided over our council in this case.

I knew that he was the instigator of all the mischief against me ; for he had never been my friend, on account of the dislike I entertained towards the customs of scalping, etc., which he, as a blood-thirsty priest, would not give up, as they helped to preserve the declining power of priest-craft. As soon as the necessary silence prevailed around the assembly, he rose and said in a solemn and mysterious voice : " Waanataa ! you are charged with conspiring against your people, the Sioux, by your connection with our enemies, the Pawnees. Defend yourself, if you can, before these warriors, who are your natural judges."

" Let first my accuser step forth !" cried I, with a resolute consciousness of my innocence. " Let me confound him, whoever he may be, as a *base liar !* "

" Well," said the haughty priest, "*I* am your accuser, and the people know that I am inspired by the Great Spirit, and cannot therefore utter an untruth."

" Then you are a base liar !" cried I, in a firm voice, "for you do not think what you now say, nor do you believe that I am guilty ; or else you would look me straight in the face as I do you. You cast down your eyes, knowing that you speak falsely, whilst I look every one here assembled into the face as an honest warrior should."

All my young fellow-warriors began to express their approbation for me, in a rather loud murmur of applause ; while older ones looked at the confounded priest, who did not utter one word in reply to what I had said against him

" Fathers and brothers," continued I, "could you ever suppose the grand-son of Waanataa to be a traitor to his people ? I have perhaps done more for my people than any warrior of my age among you. I have in a single fight vanquished Mackatana-Namakee !"

· " Black Thunder," echoed a hundred voices around me ; whilst the glance of each warrior was directed in admiration toward me for none presumed to doubt my word : except the lying priest whose face lit up with a malicious look of anticipated triumph, and who sneeringly observed :—

" Prove that you have been the vanquisher of Mackatana-Nama kee. *Show us the scalp of Black Thunder.*"

" No Sioux will ever doubt the word of a Sioux warrior ; for never a Sioux warrior was a liar ! " So saying I cast a firm look upon my false accuser, who durst not raise his eyes, while his features bespoke a suppressed rage at the outburst of applause that followed.

I now related my adventures with Diora and my fight with the
Pawnees, adding: "Fathers and brothers, you all know my antipathy to scalping and killing a vanquished and fallen foe; I would
not and could not scalp or kill Black Thunder when I had him completely in my power; but I have either by my tomahawk or my
generosity, prevented him from an invasion into our country,
which with his band he intended. Therefore, I presume to have
well deserved of my people, and I claim the reward due to me, as
to a gallant warrior. I claim the rank of a chief among you."

"Waanataa must become a chief!" cried all the young warriors in
a chorus. "Waanataa has vanquished Black Thunder! Mackatana-Namakee fell by the tomahawk of Waanataa!"

Never shall I forget that moment of triumph over my deceitful,
miserable enemy, who sat there as if he were in expectation to be
scalped. The great voting took place, and I was almost unani-
mously declared to be a chief.

In the meantime, the cunning priest had invented another plan to
destroy my life's happiness in a manner that my rank as a chief
must lose all its value to me. With an apparent resignation
to the common will of our warriors, he acknowledged their privilege
of electing me as one of their chiefs, observing that he supposed,
and expected, I would follow his example in submitting to every
other decision of the people's majority, upon which I answered that
I should certainly do so, not supposing thus to seal in advance with
my own lips the sentence of my noble Diora's death.

"Well," said he with assumed dignity, "I speak to all the Sioux—
men, women, and children. Listen to *me!* I talk to you in the
name of the Great Spirit. Is here any family who have not to mourn
at least one slain by the Pawnees, our constant irreconcilable foes?
Is here no widow who lost her husband by a Pawnee? Are here
no orphans who lost their father by a Pawnee? Is here no mother
who lost her brave son by a Pawnee? Again, is here no Sioux
warrior who has to revenge the death of a father or a son, or a brother
killed by a Pawnee?"

TERRIBLE ENCOUNTER BETWEEN THE INDIAN CHIEF AND THE HUNTER, LEROY, ON "DEVIL'S CLIFF."

Schredlicher Kampf zwischen dem Indianer-Häuptling und dem Jäger Leroy an der „Teufelsklippe.“

This abominable appeal to natural grief and national vengeance, which the cunning impostor knew thus to excite, was interrupted and answered by a general, horrible outbreak of lamentations and groans, which gradually grew.louder and louder, till they went raised to the highest possible pitch, and turned into the yells of the dreadful war-whoop.   I stood alone, unmoved and cool, in the terrible storm that surrounded me, because I thought of nothing else but the rascality of the artful priest, who continued :

"There he stands! unconcerned in your griefs and indifferent at your anger, only thinking of his love for a Pawnee squaw, the grand-daughter of Letcel and the daughter of Petaiso, called the ' *Bravest of the Braves,*' because he killed more Sioux than any other Pawnee ever did.   Listen to *me !*   I speak to you in the name of the Great Spirit.   Let her be sacrificed in memory of all the Sioux whose deaths were the triumphs of the Pawnees."

"Let her die ! let her die at the stake !" interrupted him a thousand fold echo, that struck my heart with fear which I had never felt before that moment in my life ; but my wonted courage soon returned to me, and I struggled in my mind for some calmness, to address the assembly, when Diora, who had heard every thing, broke through the door of the priest's lodge, followed by two of her guards, who both retreated when they saw me.   With one leap I was by her side, and with raised tomahawk, exclaimed, "Who dares strike Diora strikes through me.   Who will fight with Waanataa ?   Let him come forward and say he dares to raise his tomahawk against the grand son of the great Waanataa !"   None stirred, and all, even the old chiefs and warriors, remained silent, while I looked around with a calm fury which showed my resolution to fight, and to die if needs be, for my beloved wife ; but she placed her soft hand upon my mouth, and said with the true meekness of a daughter of the Great Spirit : "No bloodshed, Waanataa ; let me die for you. Diora does not fear death."   And casting a steadfast look upon the cruel homicide priest, she said in a firm and loud voice : "Prepare your stake '   I am the grand-daughter of Letcel, and the daughter

of Petalso, the Bravest of the Braves,' I will show you that I have
deserved to be Waanataa's wife, in dying for him without fear."

All sat in silence, as if they were struck by the streaked-light
from heaven; but before any of them could answer, I had seized
Diora, and carried her out of the assembly to our lodge, where my
good runner stood ready for any emergency, and mounting with
Diora, I left my country and my people, who, laboring under a
tyrannical priest-craft, would probably have sacrificed me and my
beloved wife to a wicked impostor, if we had longer exposed our-
selves to their superstition and his malignity.

Three days and nights we rode, only stopping for rest as often as
necessary for us and our horse, avoiding the Pawnee country, while
we withdrew from that of the Sioux. We were now both without
a horse.

On the morning of the fourth day we found a place fit for a longer
stay. It was a natural cave in a rock, and we were both delighted
to find running near its entrance a beautiful little spring of cold
clear water. When we had completed our little arrangements I pre
pared and left for hunting.

I was fortunate enough, as a skilful hunter, to provide an abundance before the snow fell, in which we were almost buried for some
two or three moons. In the following summer my Diora, through
the Great Spirit, gave birth to a fine and hardy son, and thus was
our happiness increased. We called our son Na-em-ceco (Child of
the Cave, Ed.)

But our solitude filled me at last with apprehension—what would
become of my wife and child were I to die? My antipathy to any
connection with other people was therefore overcome by connubial
and fatherly love; I resolved to look out for some distant neighbor
with whom I could deal to mutual advantage. Diora had no
objection to what I proposed, and leaving her well supplied with
meat. I started out, promising to return ere the falling of the first
snow. I started for the south, in order to avoid the Sioux, whom I
desired less to meet than the Pawnees After travelling along for a

time, with the aid of my faithful horse, during which time the moon changed and regained its roundness, I reached a large village of the Sac and Fox Indians, whom I supposed would be friendly toward a single and peaceable Sioux. I was unfortunately greatly mistaken in this, as they had, or presumed to have, strong reasons for consider- ing and treating every Sioux as an enemy. In their last war which they waged under " Black Eagle " against the whites, their chief was made a prisoner by a band of one hundred Sioux, who killed over eighty Sacs and Foxes in one fight, and delivered Black Eagle to the whites. In consequence of these bloody and wicked acts, peformed by a number of Sioux, the hatred of the Sac and Fox tribes fell upon all the Sioux, and as I had the misfortune of being one of the latter, although a mere boy when the circumstance occurred, I was doomed to suffer for the acts of my people who had compelled me to leave my home with them for one in the wilderness.

I had scarcely come within arrow-shot of the village when the war-whoop sounded, and in a few minutes I was surrounded by a body of their warriors. An old Fox chief made a motion of silence to his companions, who immediately obeyed him, and he said with dignity :

" Why has the Sioux dared to approach our village? Your brothers have slain many of our best warriors, and delivered our chief to our enemies. Although we have since buried the bloody tomahawk, and smoked the calumet of peace with our pale-face enemies, we have not done so with our red ones, the Sioux, who are all traitors, and therefore you shall die in sacrifice to the Great Spirit. I have spoken."

" That is right, wise and brave warrior," answered I, with a calm resignation knowing that a contradictory reply would have instantly caused my death. " If you say so, I must die; but I know that the Sacs and Foxes are great warriors and no cowards; and know that they are right in killing their enemies; I know that every traitor ought to be killed like a rattle-snake : I know that the

Sioux have been traitors to you, and that they are worse than the rattle-snakes. Now listen to me! *I am* no more a Sioux, my people have acted worse toward me and mine than they ever did to you, and I have left them never to join them again. Adopt me as your brother; give me an opportunity of proving to you my faithfulness. I have spoken!"

"Our council can alone decide upon your fate." replied the old chief. "I will neither give warrant for your veracity, because you are still a Sioux in appearance, nor will I seek to raise doubt of your sincerity, because truth shines in your face. In the meantime, till the decision of our council, you are a prisoner among us and must submit to the common treatment of such."

I was pinioned, and led through the village, like a culprit, surrounded by a body of warriors, and followed by a crowd of women and children, hooting after me, "Dog of a Sioux! Traitor! Kill him! kill him!" and throwing stones at me, and otherwise heaping indignities upon my person.

My prison was a large, miserable, decaying lodge, palisaded and continually watched by three warriors, who never answered my frequent inquiries as to the decision of my fate. How can I give you an idea of my sufferings when I thought of my wife and child? What would become of them if I returned not before the falling of the snow, and winter sun by sun drawing nearer? Agony, agony, and no other prospect of release from my prison, but a prisoner's death.

My pinions, the high palisades around my prison, and my constant three watchers, reminded me at every moment of the impossibilities of escape, and a fit of madness came over me when, with feelings of horror and despair, I beheld flakes of snow slowly falling to the ground. I groaned in my agony; and my silent watchers exchanged significant looks with each other, as if they understood my fury, which they ascribed to a mere feeling of revenge at my long captivity; they showed me their tomahawks, as if these were the only means to stop my groans and check my fury. I had repeatedly told my story, but without any success; for none of my watchers had returned, so that I supposed, at length, all the Sacs and Foxes would come successively to watch me till my death, and when the last three had had their turn to see a suffering Sioux doomed to die, they would proceed to effect their purpose.

Winter passed and spring came, while no change took place in my terrible situation: my despair became permanent, and would have turned to indifference, had it not been kept up by every thought of my poor Diora, and our dear child. I hoped against hope, that they were in a comfortable situation. Six full moons had now filled the cup of my sufferings to the brim. I had a thousand times invoked the aid of the Great Spirit to my rescue from this tomb of living misery. The scanty food which I received had reduced my strength to that of a child; when one evening the old chief, of whom I have previously spoken, came into the lodge and said: "Sioux, to-morrow you shall appear before our people." Without waiting for my answer, he left me again to my despair, as I could not guess whether or not my death was to be the topic of his people's conversation or amusement, on the following sun.

The sun was yet young when the old chief appeared again, caused my pinions to be taken off, and bade me follow him, which command I with difficulty obeyed.

A wide semi-circle of warriors was opened at our approach, and closed after we had entered. The old chief took a seat in the middle of the bow, and between other chiefs, and gave me a seat among theirs, which was so placed that they could see my face when I sat upon it. A deep silence prevailed for a few moments, but soon two men on the left wing of the semicircle began to beat upon pair of drums, to the time of which those who formed the other end of the circle commenced a council-dance.

I now thought that I was not doomed to death, although nothing else gave me the least idea of what I had to expect; for none of the features around me showed any signs of good or evil intentions, and I therefore exhibited the same apparent indifference.

The council-dance lasted about one hour, during which I was attentively observed; while only the sounds of the drums interrupted the deep silence which prevailed, and proved the solemnity of the council-dance. At its conclusion the old chief bade me rise. I did so, and he then said:—

"Sioux! Listen to me! The Sacs and Foxes are no cowards! None of us thirst after your blood, because you have behaved like a man, and not spoken a bad word against us during your long captivity; for if you had, we would have killed you in sacrifice to the Great Spirit, by whom you were led among us. You have well overcome your hard trial. Now you are free, to leave us or to join us. If you think we have wronged you, ask for satisfaction, and you shall be satisfied. Will you fight? Challenge any of us. Will you marry? Choose any one of our daughters and you shall have her. Tell us what you want, and if we can we will grant it you now. I have spoken."

"Oh, fathers and brothers," cried I, in a frenzy of despair, "give me my arms and my horse, that I may speed me to my poor wife and child, whom I left in yonder wilderness. I came hither as your friend and have become your son and brother, but you have treated me as a foe and traitor; you have confined me in your prison-lodge so long, that my poor wife and child must have perished during the winter. Let me return to my wife and child!"

My lamentations produced a visible effect on all present, and the great chief rose and offered me his sympathy. By his order, my arms and horse were immediately brought, the latter much better fed than myself. Every kind of blankets, skins, and provisions appeared in a few minutes, and about a dozen well-mounted warriors declared voluntarily their willingness to accompany me to my retreat in the wilderness, and back to their village afterwards, if I chose to return with them.

After taking a friendly leave of all, I started with my companions in search of my wife. Seven times had the moon changed its light since my separation from my beloved wife and child!

ATTEMPT TO ESCAPE. MY CAPTURE, AND CRUEL TREATMENT.

Versuch der Flucht. Meine Gefangennahme und grausame Behandlung.

Many suns had come and gone since the departure of myself and comrades, when I saw, by the appearance of the mountains in the east, that we were within a half sun's ride of my dear ones. I prevailed upon my friends to allow themselves a good night's rest—gave them the necessary information to enable them to follow me on the rise of the morrow's sun, and started with my faithful runner.

I rode on during the length of darkness without interruption, and with the sun's light I approached our cave in the rock. I saw nowhere around it any trace of a human being! Breathless I stood before the cavern's entrance; while nothing broke the silence but the violent beatings of mine own heart, as motionless I stood listening and watching for some signs of life; but I heard and saw nothing.

"Diora," whispered I, with a fainting voice; no answer. "M dear wife," said I, a little louder, but scarcely advancing a step, an trembling from head to foot, whilst chills ran through my body, and large drops of water dropped from off my forehead; still no answer! "Diora," cried I, at length, in despair. Listening again for some reply, I heard with emotions of joy my name, "Waanataa" spoken in a faint whisper. In an instant I had cleared the cavern's entrance and stood beside my own Diora.

Oh! never, never shall I think, without a shudder, of the dreadful sight which my beloved, and our dear child presented to my eyes! They were both lying upon our couch of moss, both emaciated like skeletons, both stained with blood, which filled me with intense horror, for it led me to believe that they had, in some dreadful manner, been wounded; but with feelings, none can describe, I soon discovered my mistake, for I saw the drained breast of the unhappy mother, the suckling babe with his little mouth upon her left arm, of which she had opened the artery to let him drink her life's blood, thinking that *his* life might thus be preserved, for a time, although at the sacrifice of her own, which was now nearly extinct.

When Diora cast again for the last time her sunken eyes at me,
5

her once lovely features brightened with a smile: which in its very
coming brought with it the old, handsome expression, and she
whispered, "Dear Waanataa, you have come at last, as come I knew
you would, but we must now par' forever, the Great Spirit has
called me; but he has been very good to me, for he denied me not
your presence in my last moments." I tried to close her mout'
with a kiss while thus she spoke, and with that kiss a rivulet of
tears flowed, which seemed to bear upon the bosom of its waters
my very heart, in agonizing grief, thus floating on toward the bridge
of wrecked despair.

"Dear Diora,' I managed to utter between my sobs of grief, "you
are very weak and must not talk, let me first give you drink, and
then prepare you nourishing food." I fetched some water in a
leather cup from our little spring, poured it over a handful of meal,
stirred it up with maple sugar, the two mixed with the leaves of
some berries growing near by, and presented it to my poor Diora,
who, with the natural, self-denying love of a tender mother, gave her
starving baby first to drink, before she thought of partaking herself;
while I knelt and wept, unable to further speak.

My efforts were all in vain; I could not save the lives of my
dear ones! The Great Spirit claimed them as his own. At the set-
ting sun the star of my life lost its light, became extinguished; and
in no presence, save that of the Great Spirit, I stood alone beside
the dead!

When my companions, after continuing their journey in the
moon's light, reached my cave, now a vault of death, they found
me sitting and weeping beside the inanimate bodies of her whom I
had once called Diora, and him whom we in suns past had named,
with joyous hearts, Ne-em-ecco.

My friends had the manly delicacy not to interfere in my mourn-
ing; they left me alone in my grief all the night, observing an awful silence while they lay encamped in the vicinity. Contrary to
the custom of Sioux, who generally wrap a corpse in a blanket or
skin and put it or the tops of four trees. where it decays in the

open air, I buried the bodies of my dear ones in the cave, which thus became a real vault of death. After the burial I remember no subsequent events until two moons had passed, when waking from my long fevered sleep, I found myself once more among the Fox and Sacs tribes. As soon as I regained sufficient strength I departed, refusing all proffers of friendship; and for many moons I roamed far and wide, until I at length arrived among the Brule-Sioux, with whom I have since remained. But sorrow sits deep upon my soul, life has no allurements for me, for I know not where to turn.

"Perhaps, dear Wazora" (my Indian name), said Waanataa, as he concluded his narrative, "perhaps my story has tired you?"

"Oh, no," I answered, "it has proved very interesting to me, and deeply sympathize with you in your great sorrow."

Waanataa thanked me and withdrew from the lodge. Deitosie and I remained in conversation for some time afterward, when she too left me. Shortly after her departure little Leeonoge (Temulle's young squaw) entered, and we were soon conversing in quite an animated and friendly manner, in fact Leeonoge and I had been good friends from our first acquaintance. What was my surprise to learn from her lips that Temulle intended, that very day, to take unto himself another squaw. Soon we heard the Indian drums beat, and sounds of "Kee-wan-ah" were yelled by hundreds of voices. With difficulty I almost dragged myself to the entrance of the lodge, and there for the first time witnessed an Indian marriage.

The young Indians are led, both by precept and example, to adopt the married life; and instances of celibacy very rarely continue, more particularly on the part of males, much beyond the period of mature puberty. Old bachelors, settled in their towns and villages, are a race of beings altogether unknown; I have however known a few who led a wandering life, sometimes attaching themselves to one tribe, and sometimes to another.

Early marriages are more frequent in tribes bordering on the settlements than 'n those which are more remotely situated practice is encouraged by the old men, who however say that when they were young they did not marry, nor even think of being called men, until twenty winters had passed over their heads. The intercourse with whites, they maintain, has enervated the warriors, caused the Indians to be more indolent, quarrelsome, and wicked : and materially shortened the period of their existence.

On the occasion of Temulle's marriage to his fourth wife, he walked majestically toward the North first, and then successively toward the East, South, and West. `During this time the horrible drums were fiercely beaten, yells were heard on all sides, and great excitement appeared to prevail. Then came silence, and with it the squaw to whom he was to be married, and who really was far from being an ill looking woman. *She* went through the same performance, but after walking a certain distance westward she turned, and retracing her steps about half the way, halted, and taking an ear of corn from beneath the folds of her dress, deposited it upon the ground. Temulle then walked forward, picked up the ear of corn, and amid furious yells, threw it far above him. This signified an acceptance. She went immediately up to him and seized his right wrist, and said: " Meemole is proud, happy, humble, and will do all work for the great chief Temulle." He then, in a loud voice, candidly proclaimed the warm attachment he entertained for Meemole, widow of Stameollo the warrior, and at the same time presented her with the heart of an elk (as I afterward learned), a buffalo robe, and, to my astonishment, a gold chain and locket, which I had worn before our marriage. The reader may readily imagine this whole scene as being somewhat of a sensation to me, and will I am sure forgive my weakness when it is taken into consideration that I had at least a one-fourth interest in the possession of the man thus recklessly throwing himself away. But what of that, on my own head fell the folly of my deeds ; so let us look at the next chapter, and, if possible, digest the matter therein contained

TELLS A GREAT MANY THINGS CONNECTED WITH MY LIFE AMONG THE INDIANS, AND HOW I DID NOT ESCAPE, ETC., ETC.

MEEMOLE, widow of Stameollo, brought an addition into the family besides herself. This addition was in the shape of a nine-year-old boy, who then and in after years proved one of my greatest tormentors. For instance, he would, instigated by his mother, place himself in a favorable position, and then with his toy bow and arrows (a very uncivilized specie of toy I may here remark), he would aim at any portion of my limbs which might accidentally become exposed while I attended to cooking and other domestic arrangements. I did not dare to retaliate, for such a proceeding would not have been tolerated by either his mother or step-father. Temulle had since his marriage with Meemole become a perfect tyrant, and I resolved to escape if possible. I gave up in despair being ever able to accomplish good in a missionary point of view, and therefore my religious views did not deter me from a fixed determination to immediately attempt the step.

But, in the midst of thoughts of escape, a serious accident occurred to me which bade fair to put an end to my lease of life. Whilst standing in conversation, one evening, with Deitosie and Waanataa, I felt a cold substance next the flesh of my leg, and jumping from the spot, I with a shudder heard the rattle, and beheld a rattlesnake!

At first I was thankful for my escape from the venomous bite of the reptile; but suddenly I felt a stinging sensation, and upon examination found that I had actually been badly bitten. Waanataa immediately discovered the true state of affairs, and with a spring forward he reached the rattlesnake, with one blow of his tomahawk severed its head from its body, and quickly commenced skinning and cutting it to pieces.

Meanwhile, from fright, I lay senseless. The squaws in the village soon gained intelligence of the occurrence, and were seen running about, and stooping now and then ; but Deitosie had not been idle, and was soon by my side, and with her a utensil, formed of buffalo hide, containing water and two or three handfuls of green leaves of a peculiar virtue. Meantime Waanataa had been busily engaged in placing upon the rattlesnake's bite the inner parts of the sliced pieces of its body. Each slice upon being applied to the wound would almost immediately turn black ; and just as Waanataa was about removing a third piece I awoke. This slice was only black to a small extent, and thus proved that the poison was nearly all extracted.

During the application Deitosie had poured down my throat the potion she had prepared, and afterwards she bathed my limb with it. I recovered, but my nerves undergoing another severe shock, I was again prostrated. Old Babasho, Temulle's eldest wife, in conjunction with Meemole, were my constant enemies, and left nothing undone to annoy me. I had now been with the Brule-Sioux nearly one year, and had fully resolved to escape at the first opportunity.

There occurred, however, about this time, an event which turned my thoughts back again in their old direction. This event was the appearance among us of an old Methodist preacher named John Madler, a native of New York State, and a resident of New York City ; where, I have since learned, he is quite well known. He was accompanied by a sinister looking man calling himself Maer, a Canadian-Frenchman, who came from Manitoba, over the border of Dakota.

Maer was a sort of independent trader, and remained with us some time. He related to me, with great glee, a transaction with a party of Fox Indians. These Indians were thoroughly uncivilized, and after trading every available article in his possession, excepting

CENTRING ALL MY STRENGTH IN ONE ARM, I SEVERED HIS ARM FROM HIS SHOULDER.

Mit meine Kraft in einen Arm legend, trennte ich seinen Arm von der Schulter.

his gun and ammunition, he fired it off to their intense delight, and afterwards showed them the gunpowder which caused the great noise. This, he explained, was a seed which could be planted in the ground the same as corn, and would produce a large crop They gave him many articles of value in exchange for one-half his stock of gunpowder, and he went upon his way rejoicing. Afterwards, in his trading expeditions he was careful not to trespass upon their territory, for fear the "seed" might prove an unpleasant and unprofitable harvest for him. That was *his* part of the story, but there came an unexpected sequel.

Some six months after leaving our village, he started on a trading expedition in the Blackfeet territory. He exposed his wares in one of their villages; but what was his surprise to behold some four or five Indians walk up and carry off all his property. He laid his complaint before the chief, who informed him that the Indians, who had his property, were honest Fox who had joined his tribe, and that they promised to pay their white brother when the *black seed grew.*

Rev. John Madler and I had many warm religious conversations. He spoke hopefully of making many converts among the Indians. He denounced in strong terms the habit, so prevalent among the whites, of breaking nearly all their treaties with the red men, which caused the latter to harbor nothing but distrust in their dealings with the sons of civilization. With great earnestness he besought me to walk without fear in the path that I had chosen; and reminded me that good could not be accomplished without some sacrifice. In fact so strong were his arguments, that I decided to remain in my present position; and again resolved upon rigidly following out my early missionary intentions.

Mr. Madler remained with us three weeks. He spoke the Sioux dialect quite fluently; and possessing fine oratorical powers, he was listened to with great respect by our tribe, but his religious enthusiasm was, I am sorry to say, without its intended effect. He certainly gained the respect of our tribe, but they would not accept

his truths, for, said they, "The pale faces were sent upon earth by
the Evil Spirit, who was at a loss for some plan to vex us, and so
conceived the idea of sending us whites that they might rob us of
our territory, and leave us nothing in exchange but fire-water, to
madden our brains and destroy our bodies." This was their theory,
and nothing which the Rev. Madler could advance in opposition to
it, would in any way combat their ideas. "You are good pale face
to-day," they said, "but to-morrow's sun may see thee bad pale face,
for we have seen, we cannot but know."

It was the eve of Mr. Madler's departure, and that of his companion, Maer. We had been sitting outside the door of our lodge.
I had just related the incident of the snake bite, and mentioned the
leaves which Deitosie had used as a remedy. Maer expressed a
great desire to gather some, in which Mr. Madler also joined.

Deitosie, who was present, volunteered to show them a spot, but
a short distance from the village, where they grew in abundance.
Tcmulle had been absent some two or three days, and not fearing his
displeasure, I also volunteered to accompany the party. The moon
shone brightly that night, as we set forth upon our botanical trip.
We had proceeded something over half a mile from the village,
when, quick as thought, Maer with a furious blow struck Mr. Madler to the ground, and turning dealt Deitosie one equally as hard.
Before I could gather my senses he had completely enveloped my
head and shoulders in his cloak, thus stifling all cries for help,
which I might have given vent to. Seizing me in his strong arms
he ran quickly forward. I heard the neighing of a horse near by, and
soon felt myself lifted upon its back, and knew that Maer was there
beside me. The villain had planned the whole affair and soon the
horse was galloping on at a pushed speed. My thoughts during
this time were of an unenviable kind. What object could he have
this abduction? Madman, did he not realize that we should
soon be pursued and overtaken.

We had probably gone some ten or fifteen miles before he reined
up. He dismounted and lifted me from the horse's back. Then a

long silence ensued, which was at length broken by shouts from Maer, and sounds of a switch descending upon the back of the horse, a neigh of terror from the animal, and then as of some heavy body rolling down a ravine.

The cloak was then withdrawn from my head, and I in a half insensible manner regained my power of speech, and looked around me. There stood Maer with the face of a demon, his eyes bloodshot and a ghastly smile on his unprepossessing countenance.

"You are now the wife of Maer. Do you not comprehend me?" he said.

I could make no reply.

"You don't mind it, eh? Good! Well, I will tell you something. In a short time those red-skin devils will be upon us. Arriving at this spot they will notice something unusual, and will trace that something to the edge of this ravine, down which I caused my horse to leap. They will suppose us to have been on the horse when he went down. Now, in order to reach the bottom, they will be obliged to retrace their steps some eight miles. During that time, and that which we have gained in advance of them, we can walk a little ways—can't we, my dear? and after we do walk a little ways I know a nice little hiding place. Now aint I a schemer? It's all for you, too!"

The villain evidently considered that I did not object to his plans, and knowing my helplessness, I concluded for the present not to undeceive him. So on we went, until we arrived at the banks of a small stream. Before emerging from the woods, Maer removed his moccasons and desired me to do the same. He then procured four large pieces of wancton bark. Two of these pieces he tied to his feet, one under each foot. The other two pieces he tied to mine. We then started for the stream; after reaching which we untied our "bark shoes," and walked down the brook.

How far we walked I have no idea; but at last in an exhausted condition, my feet badly swollen, we reached a hut, or lodge, of peculiar construction Upon our arrival, there appeared at the

door, gun in hand, a strange looking creature, whom one could
scarcely name a man. His legs were twisted in a manner such as I
have never seen possessed by a human being. One shoulder was
drawn high up above the other; and his eyes, which cannot be
described as being of any known color, were overhung by eyebrows
of great thickness. One arm was, or appeared to be, much longer
than the other; and a more singular looking object, in the shape of
man, could not be found.

" Ah, this is my true friend, Red Rappo," said Maer, and added
he, aside, " he is a sort of half-breed. His father was a Blackfeet,
and his mother was, well there's no knowing exactly what, only she
was not an Indian ;" and, added he, this time addressing the creature
before him :—

" Rappo, we are hunted by Sioux, and would hide, show us to
your cave beneath the Anonmaho."

" I see a friend," answered the strange being thus addressed, " and
will serve him. Serve him falsely, never. Come ! "

Into the hut we followed Red Rappo. Looking round me I could
see no other entrance save the one through which we came. The
lodge or hut was built against a large rock, the sides of which served
for the wall at the back. Rappo went directly to the wall and
pushing it in a peculiar manner several times, a large stone fell,
leaving a hole large enough for one person at a time to crawl
through. Maer bade me enter first. This I objected to, expressing
a fear as to what might meet me beyond. At this both Rappo and
the Canadian laughed, the latter informed me that there was nothing
to fear, as we were about entering a natural cave. Knowing that
further objections might cost me my life I reluctantly entered,
followed by Maer, who, when inside, raised the stone to its former
position. We walked through a dark cave for some distance, when
we suddenly came to a lighted torch placed in a notch in the rocks.
Here, to my surprise, I beheld a running brook. Maer, who appeared to be perfectly familiar with his surroundings, retraced his
steps, but before leaving me, told me to venture no further, as to do

so would be certain death. He said that in less than half an hour he should return. and then all would be well.

Moved by some incomprehensible power I walked quite a ways from the spot upon which my abductor had left me. Want of courage caused me to stop. I then contemplated the hopeless position in which I was placed, and preferred death to remaining in the power of the villain Maer. I continued to advance, slowly and cautiously, through the underground brook, which was scarcely knee-high. I walked probably half a mile. when with a prayer to God, and renewed courage I kept upon my uncertain way. Suddenly I bethought myself of the torch burning in the notch, and feeling assured that its possession by me would be of great value, I went back to my starting point, obtained the light, and almost ran the distance I had walked before. The splashing water echoed and re-echoed throughout the cave. I desperately fought the feeling of fear within me, and determined to continue, even if death should be the consequence; on, on I went.

I know not the distance I had traversed after obtaining the torch, but suddenly a thousand lights danced before my eyes; and all the fairy tales that I had read in my childhood seemed about to be verified. 'Twas as if all the rubies, and precious stones of the world, were imbedded in the rocks around me; and in an ecstasy of wonder and delight I paused to view this scene of gorgeousness. But suddenly I was reminded of my perilous situation, and the immediate necessity for action; so on I went, carefully searching for signs of danger.

I must have gone several miles, when, to my great joy, I beheld an opening beyond. With hastened steps I walked toward it, and upon my arrival was met by an unexpected difficulty. The brook rushed down the rocks at a height of full two hundred feet; and upon neither side could I find means of exit from the cave. I stood gazing upon this truly grand work of nature, and fully resolved, that in case of pursuit, I would jump into the basin beneath. knelt and sent up a prayer to God, and there upon my knees, I

thought of my past life, reviewed it calmly, and with a resigned
mind, awaited my fate. In the midst of such thoughts I was
aroused by a great splashing sound, and turning found myself in
the arms of Maer. His face was covered with blood, and from a
hole in his forehead the blood was slowly trickling down. His expression I shall never forget, as with an oath he seized me, and
hissed into my ear these words :—

"You thought to escape me, my beauty, did you ? But I have
you now, despite the endeavors of that canting preacher to trick
me of my prize. Curse him ! He shall pay for every drop of
blood I have lost. Thought to kill me, did he ? And I do believe
Rappo is dead, shot by that hellish squaw. Come, we must get away
from here."

So saying he dragged me back towards the entrance to the cave,
reaching which he pushed me through the hole in the rock, and
quickly followed. As I gained my feet upon the floor of the cabin
I beheld Deitosie, who was about to spring forward to meet me,
when seeing the head and shoulders of Maer emerging from the
cave, she darted toward him instead, and seizing him dragged him
through, and administed a sound beating to his Canadian majesty. •
But once firmly upon his feet he would have proved too much for
her; but fortunately, at this critical moment, good Mr. Madler appeared upon the scene, and by a well-directed blow from the butt
of his gun, succeeded in rendering our antagonist powerless, and
without uttering a sound he fell to the floor.

I now observed that Mr. Madler's left arm hung upon a strip of
linen suspended from his neck. This was all duly explained to me
As soon as Mr. Madler recovered his senses, after being knocked
down by Maer, near the Sioux village, he ran back, and (crazy from
the unexpected circumstances attending our walk, and a severe pain
in the head, occasioned by Maer's blow,) mounted the first horse he
came to, without giving any particulars to the Indian who stood near
him, and galloped furiously away.

Arriving at the spot where he had left Deitosie insensible, he

THE MANNER IN WHICH THE SIOUX INDIANS DISPOSE OF THEIR DEAD IN THE TOPS OF TREES.

Die Art und Weise der Sioux-Indianer, sich ihrer Todten zu entledigen — in den Wipfeln der Bäume.

found her standing up, and when she saw him she begged to accompany him. So the two thus mounted rode on, little knowing where,
but, directed by a kind and all-seeing Providence, they came upo*
Rappo's hut. Standing in the door was Maer, who upon seeing
them fired his gun, the ball from which took effect in Mr. Madler's
left arm.

With great effort Mr. Madler returned the shot, and fortunately it
also took effect, for Maer put his hand to his forehead and disappeared within. Rappo now came to the front and fired, but with no
effect, his ball passing harmlessly by. Rev. Madler had now dropped his gun,, and was attending to his wound, which had become
by this time exceedingly troublesome. Deitosie with great firmness
picked up the fallen gun and fired. The smoke cleared away, and
Rappo lay dead! Mr. Madler then seized the gun, and rushing
forward fearlessly entered the cabin; but to his surprise, and that
of Deitosie, who had followed him, Maer was nowhere to be seen
He and the Indian maiden searched everywhere, but without suc
cess, and they had given up all hopes of being able to rescue me.
Madler had just left the hut for the fourth or fifth time, and Deitosie
had stood near the door wonderingly, when my appearance, fol
lowed by that of Maer, and the attending consequences, took place

Deitosie and myself were seated upon the horse's back, and with
great thankfulness we wended our way toward our village, accompanied by good Mr. Madler. About half way we were met by a
large body of mounted Sioux warriors, who in surprise greeted our
arrival. The story was soon told, and Rev. Madler was the hero, and
Deitosie the heroine of the day.

Two days afterward Mr. John Madler set out upon his journey.
accompanied by an "Anee" (bachelor) Indian who had formed a
warm attachment for him. With the good doctor I in sorrow
parted, but cheerfully remarked that we should meet again.

"If not in this world, then in the next," he said.

Shortly after this commenced a series of persecutions beyond
Christian forbearance. Maer, the trader, had left a quantity of the

6

worst whiskey ever distilled, and nearly all the Indians partook
freely of it; Temulle among the rest. After drinking a quantity
of the poisonous liquid he would come to the lodge, and ordering me
out would devise all sorts of plans for his own amusement. Some
I dare not mention, but others I will. At one time he came to m
and said that the council had ordered me to swim the river, which
was near the village. Accordingly I was seized by two squaws, who
forced me toward the river, followed by Indians, both men and
women, in a beastly state of intoxication. Arrived at the river, my
tormentors waded out, dragging me with them. Fortunately they
had hold of the wrong person to gratify them in the manner they
desired, as I was an expert swimmer and readily swam to the opposite bank. Finding that they were foiled in their intentions regarding myself, the male Indians forced all the squaws, who had accompanied us, into the river, where they were followed and forced into
deep water. Some five or six of the women could not swim, and
of these three were drowned, to the great amusement of the drunken
wretches on shore.

At another time, Temulle, still under the influence of liquor,
whipped me severely, and then painted my face with the blood
which ran from the wounds upon my body. His passion for tor-
menting me was at its height, when fortunately for me, but unfortunately for others, two teamsters were brought in as prisoners.
And—why need dwell upon the horrible scene?—these men were tied
to the stake, and surrounded by howling, drunken Indians, they
were burned to death.[1]

Not long after this terrible affair, two white girls were brought to
our village and forced to take braves as husbands or die at the stake.
From them I learned a sad history of Indian cruelties. Their name
was Howson. Three years previous the father, John W. Howson,
and his wife and three children, from Kentucky, had sought and
found a home in the far West. Everything had prospered, and in
their happy home few thoughts of evil came. But the destroyer
was on their track. One day there came seven Indians who

exhibited every sign of peaceable intentions. They asked for food and received it. After stuffing themselves to their hearts' content they asked for fire-water. Mr. Howson and his wife, who were both in the house, informed them that he had none, in fact neve' used it.

"White man lie!" said one of the Indians, "and me kill him, he no give us fire-water."

Mr. Howson still persisting that there was nothing of that kind in the house, the Indians rushed upon, and struck him to the ground, where they scalped him alive before the eyes of his distracted family. Mrs. Howson, an invalid, unable to move from her chair, sat wring-ing her hands and calling for mercy. The Indians, now thoroughly maddened at the sight of blood, next directed their attention toward a boy of about four years of age, and one tall powerful brute took him by the heels and dashed his brains out against the door post. The daughters, Annie and Lizzie, had fainted at this horrible sight, and when they became conscious their home was in ashes, and their mother buried beneath. The Indians who committed this dastardly deed were of the Lo tribe. but they brought their captives to our village.

Lizzie Howson was a very pretty *blonde*, and her sister Annie a *brunette* of rare beauty. All my sympathies were enlisted in their favor; but what could I do to aid them? Nothing, absolutely nothing, for *I* was a captive in reality. Thoughts of escape, with-out any fixed plan to accomplish it, were again running through my mind, and—well, the next chapter will let you into several secrets and uform you to several adventures of mine.

CHAPTER VI

THE ESCAPE—CAPTURED AND BROUGHT BACK—WHIPPED—CON-
DEMNED TO DEATH AT THE STAKE—INTERCESSION OF WAANATAA.

ONE evening Deitosie and I had walked a short distance beyond the village, and our conversation at length turned
upon the cruelties of my husband Temulle. To her I expressed a desire to quit forever the Brule tribe, and she
volunteered to accompany me anywhere. So we sat down
and arranged our plans for escape. It was decided that we should
make some excuse the next day, which would admit of a long
absence, without creating any suspicion as to our real intentions.

We determined upon taking with us a good supply of provisions
and our destination was Red Rappo's hut. There we could hide in
the cave, with safety, until all pursuit of us had been abandoned,
for now that Maer and Rappo were dead, the secret of the cave was,
we felt sure, known to but three persons—Deitosie, myself, and Dr.
Madler.

Everything favored us the following day, for Temulle went on a
hunt, in the opposite direction from that which we intended taking;
and so, bright and early, we started with the avowed purpose of
herb gathering. Arriving at the banks of the stream (which I have
before mentioned), I removed my moccasons, and caused Deitosie to
do the same. Then, as did Maer, when he and I were there before,
I procured the pieces of bark, and hid our trail. We waded
through the brook until we came to Red Rappo's hut, and here we
were greeted by a horrible sight. Locked in each other's arms,
were the now inanimate bodies of Rev. Madler and the Canadian Maer.
Close by lay the body of the Indian, who had accompanied the
doctor, shot through the head.

H1

Here was a mystery, the only solution of which we could arrive at, being, that Maer was not dead when we left him, and had afterwards met Mr. Madler and his guide, shot the latter, and with the former closed in deadly combat. With all the nerve at our command we removed the bodies from the lodge, and with a sickening sensation managed to crawl into the cave. Once inside, we were puzzled to adjust the stone which filled the entrance; but after great exertion we managed to arrange it in its proper place.

Deitosie followed me, not without some fear however, through the cave until we came to the underground brook, when, to my surprise, I found a torch brightly burning, and placed in the same notch where I had seen and taken the other. What could this mean? A terror shook my limbs, but I did not wish to mention the fact to my companion. Strange thoughts ran through my brain; and to all questions asked by Deitosie I returned but indifferent answers.

Frantically I seized the torch and rushed forward. I had not gone far when, with a scream, I started back, for there directly in front of us, his eyes like balls of fire, *stood Red Rappo!* Both Deitosie and myself lost all possession of our limbs and senses, and sank unconscious into the running water beneath us. Happily the water had an immediate sanitary effect, and with choking sensations we found our senses returning. We managed, by clinging to each other, to stand, but neither could utter a sound, and still before us *stood Red Rappo!* What horrible expression he had. How awfully weird looked he; and as I gazed in stony horror at the picture presented, it

"Filled me, thrilled me, with a terror never felt before."

With a prayer to God, I regained somewhat my wonted self-possession, and in a voice weak with fear I managed to utter:—

'Rappo, we come not to harm you. We are but two helpless women; have mercy, have mercy!"

No sound, save the noise occasioned by the running water greeted us. He is waiting to spring upon us! He would amuse

himself at our fright! Soon he will rend us limb from limb!
Some such wild thoughts presented themselves to my now crazed
brain, and with them came the feeling of faintness again.   My companion stood like a bronze statue, nor uttered she one word.

With no belief in things supernatural, the idea slowly crept in
upon me that we were looking at the spirit of Red Rappo.   I gained
at length, sufficient courage to advance a few steps.   As I did so I
bade the object before us to come forward, if he were man or spirit.
But there staring at us, with a look that chilled my very blood,
stood Red Rappo!   Suddenly yells were echoed throughout the
cave.   What meant those shouts?   Whence did they proceed?
With feelings none can describe, I turned to my companion, who by
this time had regained her power of speech.

Our people have found, and followed our trail," she said.

Again the yells were sounded in our ears, and the truth soon
became apparent to me.   Rushing forward, I know not why, I ran
against the object which had caused us so much terror, and as I did
so it fell—'twas the body of Red Rappo.   Here was another mys
tery.   Holding the torch high above my head I beheld a hole near
where the body had been placed, and, on examination, I found
another cave adjoining the one we were in.   Hurriedly _ bade
Deitosie follow me, and soon I found myself in a cavern of huge
dimensions.   A large rock lay at our feet, and, with the as tance
of the Indian maiden, we, upon trial, found it to exactly fit the hole
through which we had crawled.   We had scarcely been in our new
hiding place a minute, when we heard the echo of voices, and the
tramping of many feet in the adjoining cave.

Three days and nights, I should judge, we passed in this cavern
Often we heard voices and other sounds, but our hiding place
remained undiscovered by our pursuers.   At last, weary of our con-
finement we concluded to carefully advance along the cavern.   Our
torch had burned to its last knot, and, in the darkness, we were
obliged to grope our way.   It is a singular fact that the air of this
cave was not, as far as we could judge from our feelings, the least

COUNCIL DANCE OF THE SAC AND FOX INDIANS. — Rath8-Tanz der Sac und Fox-Indianer.

tut impure. We were reduced in provisions to one piece of cooked beef steak weighing about two pounds. Fear prevented us from re' ·rning the way we came, even if we had been able to find the entrance, which is doubtful, and our situation was desperate. T remain was certain starvation, and so out we were obliged to go But how? Was there an exit to this cave? We pushed hopefully on, knowing not what was before us. At any moment we might be plunged down some deep abyss. Oh, it was terrible, but there was no help for it, so on, on we went.

We had traversed the cavern a great while when we suddenly beheld before us what appeared to be a star of heaven. Towards it we went, and after walking quite a distance came to a hole scarcely large enough to admit a person to crawl through. I first reached out far enough to take a view of its surroundings, when with feelings of despair I beheld, directly to the right of me, the self same brook, rushing down the rocks, which I had before seen in the other cavern. But joy! joy, to the left of me I saw a ledge of rock upon which we, with care, could crawl. I told Deitosie of my discovery, and crawled out, followed soon after by my companion.

The rock upon which we stood was some one hundred and fifty w. two hundred feet above the plain beneath us. Deitosie, after walking around some time, came to me with the news that to the left of us was a natural path by which we could descend.

With great difficulty, we managed, at last, to reach the valley and with thankful hearts we knelt, I with a prayer, which was repeated by the Indian maiden. After a long rest we rose to our feet and had walked some distance, when we heard the sound of wheels belonging evidently to heavy emigrant wagons, and soon after we met a party of twenty men, and with them three wagons and twelve horses. I entered into conversation with them and warned them to go to the extreme right, as our people would, in all probability, engage them in battle under some pretence, and rob them of everything. They were pleased to learn that I was the wife of Temulle (or Squatting Bear as they called him), told me they were on their way, with supplies, to Fort Berthald, and wished to stop at the Brule village. I did not like to own that I was then attempting to escape from my husband, and therefore, after again repeating my warning, at which they only laughed, I left them to go their way. They had been gone about half an hour when who should suddenly appear before us but Temulle. The game was up! It had been fairly played, but our antagonist held the winning card.

Without a word Temulle pointed toward the Brule village, and I, in company with my companion, led the way, followed closely by Temulle.

Arrived at the village, we were hailed by the Indians with all 'sorts of exclamations, and I was glad to get into the lodge, to escape their taunts. But my trouble was by no means at an end. Temulle walked in soon after and whipped me so severely that I expected nothing short of death to ensue. Not content with this he pounded me with his fists, until, overcome by such treatment, I fainted. Nor was this all, for in the morning I awoke to learn that the council, then more than half crazy with liquor, had condemned me to be burned at the stake.

All my Christian fortitude was required to bear up under these trials.

The time appointed for the sacrifice, as the Indians termed it, arrived, and with trembling limbs, but a strong faith in God, I walked forth to meet my doom. Tied to the stake I waited the signal that would start the flames around me. The sky was dark with clouds, heavy winds were blowing, when suddenly vivid flashes of lightning illumined the heavens above. Waanataa now appeared upon the scene, and addressed the Indians. He bade them beware of the Great Spirit's wrath. They were about to burn a woman who had never harmed them, and the Great Spirit would talk to them. As he spoke a loud peal of thunder rent the air, and the Indians dropped as if struck by some unseen power. There I stood a witness to this scene of so much import to myself.

The elements were now let loose in all their fury. The wind blew, a perfect hurricane, peal after peal crashed as if in contention with some great antagonist, and the vividness of the lightning clearly exposed each object to view, when suddenly the earth trembled, then shook and shook again, till with one mighty heave it seemed to throw off all the weight upon it, and the next flash of lightning showed the land not far off, to be split as far as the eye could reach. During these events Waanataa could be seen standing erect, calm and collected.

Presently the storm abated, and Waanataa walked up to the stake and severed the cords which bound me, and then, turning to the Indians, huddled together like sheep, he said:

"Sioux, the Great Spirit has spoken, and do you not know what the lightning was saying?"

After the storm had passed over I went to my lodge, and there offered up a prayer of thanksgiving for my rescue from death.

Temulle, for some time subsequently, treated me with great respect, as did also the rest of the tribe, but this soon wore off, and again did I submit to seemingly never-ending persecutions.

The following day a white man approached the village on horse-back, and informed us that he was one of a party *en route* for Fort Berthald. He it was with whom I had conversed and warned not to enter the Brule village.

After great parley he was ordered to bring his companions before the chief, and accordingly did so, when commenced a general massacre, only one of the party escaping to tell the tale.

Things in the neighborhood were getting too hot for a longer stay on the part of the Sioux, and owing to the late murders and depredations, they knew that the pale-faces would soon be on the trail as avengers, and consequently after a council had been held, it was agreed that the best policy would be to "pull up stakes" and leave.

The Indians generally act upon impulse, and in a short time our tribe was on the move, and the deserted village lay far behind. For days we travelled, and I, the "noble Indian's wife," was obliged to

bear my pack with the other squaws. At length we arrived at Mine
Wakan Lake, where we remained but a short time, fearing pursuit,
and then struck across the border, avoiding Manitoba, however. Our
course now lay along the Assiniboin river, on the banks of which
we encamped several days. A few miles from the banks of the
Assiniboin river, a hut, occupied by an Indian of the Blackfeet tribe,
was discovered, and from him Temulle obtained another supply of
whiskey, and then again commenced the deviltries previously practised, and as I was about the only object to practise upon, " your
humble servant " was the instrument used for his amusement.

Temulle was at his wits' end for some new amusement, when he
conceived the idea of dressing Meemole and myself in male costume
that of the braves, and placing us face to face in deadly combat.
So after being obliged to dress as directed, I was brought forward
and confronted by Meemole, dressed in a similar manner, and who -
judging by the smile of satisfaction she wore, seemed inclined to
enjoy the thing immensely. I remonstrated, but to no effect, and
was told that Meemole had orders to kill me whether I fought or
not. Out of all the Indians present but three stood by me. as
champions: these three were Waanataa, Deitosie, and little
Leeonoge. Deitosie begged Temulle to allow her to take my place,
and even little Leeonoge expressed a wish to " go right up and
kill bad squaw."

The idea of this Amazonian encounter tickled the Indians immensely, and with sinking heart, I saw that there was no help for
it, I must either kill or be killed. I did not relish the idea of
human blood upon my hands, nor was I inclined to sit calmly by
and receive the knife of my bitter enemy.

Meemole had, since her marriage, left no means undone to annoy
me, and all my sufferings both at her hands and those of Temulle,
gave her the greatest delight, but I trust the kind reader will credit
me when I assert that no feelings of revenge toward her had ever
possessed me.

Waanataa came and in a whisper, advised me to stand up bravely and fight it out, for "she is not likely to kill you," he said, and if you watch your opportunity and seize with a firm hand her right wrist, and cut her slightly across the stomach the victory is yours. Nothing," he added, "will cause greater fear in such an encounter than a cut on that particular part of the body. I have known braves to receive severe, and sometimes death wounds, in more vital parts, and continue fighting, not knowing that they were badly cut, whilst at other times I have seen them conqured by a little scratch across the stomach."

Knowing that Waanataa, next to Deitosie, stood my best friend, I decided to act upon his advice.

It is perhaps necessary, though I hesitate through modesty, in asserting it, to state that I am what is termed a *well made woman.* Brought up in the country, and having at the same time a desire to avail myself of the exercise which may there be obtained, g.on .. be a strong girl, and at fifteen there were few of the boys in our neighborhood who cared to test my strength—in fact, I was at that age a perfect "tom boy."

My opponent, in this contest, possessed a well knit body, and no doubt we were equally matched.

And now came preparations for the "tug of war." Face to face we stood, knives in hand. On her face malice, and a fixed look which boded me no good. Upon my face there was, I am sure, an expression of determination. I resolved not to kill her unless pushed to do so in self-defence. The signal to commence hostilities was given, and quick as lightning Meemole sprang forward, and before I was aware of it, gave me a severe cut across the face with her knife. For a moment I was bewildered, but remembering my danger, and I may truly say, my American blood being up, I went in for dear life. My first effort was to seize her right wrist, which fortunately I succeeded in doing, but she too had learned that trick, and so I found myself *non-combattant.* Now commenced a struggle for supremacy. Locked in each other's arms, we neither of us could use the knife. At last with an effort I threw my antagonist, and as

she fell she pulled me with her, leaving me however "on top."
Several Indians now stepped forward and separated us, and we were
commanded to stand upon our feet, which we did, and having learned
a lesson from Meemole at the commencement of the encounter, I proceeded immediately to put it to practical use, and this time it was
her turn to receive the cut upon the face.

The quickness with which I accomplished this served to call forth
the applause of the drunken Indians, and Meemole in no manner
relishing this good opinion of my powers, rushed forward, the blood
streaming from her face, with the fury of an enraged tigress. The
blade of her knife clashed against mine, and centring all my
strength in the one arm, I threw my antagonist off. Again she
came at me, and, acting on the defensive, I backed a step or two,
and she in miscalculating the distance would have fallen, had I not
instantly seized her, and doing so we both fell.

This time there was no interference, and we rolled over and over,
cutting and slashing at each other in a manner which appeared to be
terrible, but which was in reality of no great effect, except to start
a considerable quantity of blood. Temulle at last, seeing that I was
getting the best of the squaw, ordered us to be separated. Again
we stood face to face, and a sorry appearance we must have presented.
Meemole had decidedly the worst of it, but her courage was by no
means gone, and it bade fair to be a long and deadly encounter.
She lost no time in acting on the offensive, and it was with great
difficulty that I avoided several savage thrusts, any one of which, I
doubt not, would have proved fatal to my existence. Many times
had I attempted the "cut" which Waanataa advised me to make,
but without success.

My antagonist was now becoming weak from loss of blood, and in
her despair was fighting wildly, and in such a manner that I could
not have longer warded off her stabs, had not fortune at last favored
me, for in another attempt I succeded in grasping Meemole's wrist,
and quick as thought, dealt her a cut across the stomach, which
thoroughly unnerved her, and *the victory was mine !*

Weak from loss of blood, and unnerved through excitement, I was carried, by Waanataa, to my lodge, the Indians making way for us, and on every side my courage was lauded to the skies. In a day or two I had sufficiently recovered to be able to assist in the care of my late enemy, Meemole, who was very grateful, and ever afterward remained a true and firm friend of mine.

The Indian previously mentioned as living a few miles from the Assiniboin river, came to our encampment two or three days after the Amazonian contest, and having heard of it, he expressed a great partiality toward me.

One day as I wandered a short distance from our temporary village, I was met by the Indian trader, and his attentions becoming of too free a nature to satisfy my sense of propriety, I started to leave him, but he detained me, and despite my endeavors to escape him, carried me to his hut. We had scarcely arrived there, when Temulle made his appearance, and then commenced a hand to hand encounter between these two red men, in which however my husband had decidedly the best of his antagonist, and soon overpowered him. Temulle then bound him hand and foot, and dragged him to the village, where he was roasted alive. The Brules afterward confiscated his property, and burned his hut to the ground.

Not far from our encampment Waanataa discovered a cave or seemingly a tomb, in which were found skulls and skeltons of a race of Indians long since extinct. The shortest one of these skeletons could not have been less than seven feet nine in length, and several of them actually measured over eleven feet. Tomahawks of queer shapes, pipes of peculiar make, and other articles were found in abundance, one of which, an ornament cut from a solid block of gold, I still have in my possession.

It would be impossible to narrate in one volume the many exciting events of my life during my five years' sojourn among the Indians, but I have in contemplation the compilation of another book of this size which will be comprised of adventures among the Cheyenne tribe, which tribe I have a greater respect for than that which I

7

entertain for the Brule-Sioux. During my life among the latter, I met and conversed with Spotted Tail and many other well known Indians. In the month of August, 1872 (the year of my return), I was on a visit to New York city, and again met and conversed with Spotted Tail, and his squaw, who, by the way, is a sister to the " Little Leeonoge," of whom I have spoken.

Our tribe was on the move for a long while, and during that time we visited the winter Trading Post, Blackfeet territory, having travelled along a very beautiful little river known as the Mouse, afterwards striking the Plum river. We were at one time near Fort Ellice, and thence along the Qu Appelle river, and afterwards stop- ped at the Qu Appelle Post. We spent some time on the Fishing Lakes among the Blackfeet Indians, and again along the Red Deer river to Cache Camp, taking in Old Bow Fort *en route*. During this time I was to a great extent thoroughly resigned to my situation Temulle had for a long time acted toward me in a manner more lenient than during the first two years of our marriage, but suddenly a complete change took place in his disposition, and again I was subject to such cruel treatment that I firmly resolved to escape. Early in the spring we returned to Dakota territory, and afterwards went with the greater portion of our tribe into the State of Minnesota. Here were renewed those cruelties which I have before mentioned.

One day there came to our camp an old hunter named Darrel Leroy. I seized the first opportunity to speak to this man of my desire to leave the Indians, and he promised that if it ever lay in his power to assist me he should not hesitate to render me aid.

Temulle, on one occasion, had just given me a severe whipping, when there came to the village an old Brule chief, who had been for many years among the Blackfeet. He witnessed the scene between my husband and myself. Without flinching I had received the whipping administered by Temulle, and he seemed to enjoy my suffering. At the conclusion he offered Temulle a pony in exchange for the 'white squaw.' This offer being refused he next offered two, and then three ponies, and for *three ponies my noble* (?) *Indian*

husband handed me over to Mackamoze, the old Brule chief, who
that very day set out for a neighboring tribe, accompanied by an
' Anee " friend. I bade good bye to Deitosie, Waanataa and Little
Leeonoge (the latter was then in a dying condition), and followed my new
"proprietor." Daniel Leroy, the old hunter, did not even come forward to bid me farewell, but kept decidedly aloof.

We had been on our way two days, and had probably travelled
some forty odd miles, when we struck a small stream called the "Naog"
(roaring) brook. Mackamoze expressed it as his intention to remain
here some three or four days. We had scarcely been upon the spot
selected an hour when Daniel Leroy rode up, having the three ponies
given Temulle by the old chief, with him. He entered into a conversation with Mackamoze, the substance of which was that he desired
to buy me back. He offered the three ponies and other presents,
and promised the old chief "much money " if he would accompany
us to one of the forts after the trade.

Nothing however would induce Mackamoze to trade for me, and he
and the other Indian took possession of the three ponies and bade the
hunter leave them instantly under pain of death. They asserted that
Leroy had stolen the ponies.

In vain did he deny the charge and assert that he had paid
Temulle for them. At last in desperation he struck down the
" Anee " with the butt end of his gun, and turning instantly, pointed
the muzzle of it toward Mackamoze, ordering him to stand or be shot
down in his tracks. The old chief rushed forward—Leroy pulled
the trigger—the gun missed fire, and dropping it, he seized Mackamoze, and then came a struggle for supremacy. For a long time
neither could throw the other. At length they both fell heavily
to the ground.

Over and over they rolled, both adepts in the tricks of a hand to
hand encounter. It was a prolonged contest. Blood flowed freely
from each. With a great struggle Leroy succeeded in shaking off
his antagonist, and in a moment was on his feet. But not before the
who was up and ready to meet him again. They clinched,

and the struggle was again desperately renewed. Near, very near to them was the mouth of a yawning abyss. I called to Leroy, warning him of his danger, but, alas, too late, for a few steps backward carried the Indian over the edge, and in his fall he clung to the buck-skin jacket of his adversary, thus dragging the old hunter with him. They disappeared from my sight. With terror I rushed to the edge of the abyss, and there hung Leroy, his legs twisted around a wancton tree, which grew on a ledge of rock, and still clinging to him was the Indian chief. The strength of Leroy seemed superhuman, for as he hung he managed with one hand, by seizing the tree, to steady himself, whilst with the other he repeatedly stabbed his antagonist, who, with a yell of agony, let go his hold, and went crashing down on the rocks below.

Leroy found great difficulty in regaining an upright position after the Indian had let go his hold; but at last, with what assistance I could render, he accomplished the feat, and after a rest we started toward the white settlements, where, after several days' journey we arrived completely exhausted.

I soon found friends enough, who dressed me in "civilized costume," and I was shortly afterward on my way to Fort Leavenworth, and remaining there but a short time, I started for the good Old Bay State.

During my stay among the Brule-Sioux, William Welsh, Esq., made an official visitation among the Indians, and afterward made some wise and good suggestions in his report. He gave an interesting account of the social and religious condition of the various tribes, and urges the more thorough carrying out of the principle that when a civilized people deprive the uncivilized possessors of the soil of their food and clothing, the civilized people are bound to subsist and clothe the uncivilized until they can support themselves. Mr Welsh also recommends the United States Government to adopt more effective measures for the prohibiton of the whiskey traffic among the Indians, and in that recommendation I too join an earnest prayer for the total prohibition of the damning fluid among those

savage creatures, for two thirds of the murders and wars among
themselves and against the whites are committed under its influence,
and to the other *third* we can but add that it's man's inhumanity to
the red-man.   ———

If my narrative has proved interesting I am well satisfied, but if
in its perusal some silly girl may change her mind regarding the
noble red men and relinquished all thoughts of going among them,
for any purpose whatever, then am I fully satisfied.

CHAPTER VII.

HAVE, since my return, been importuned by numerous friends
and acquaintances, to give to the public some of the receipts
in use among the Indians, for the cure of diseases. The publishers of this work, knowing the great value of these receipts.
gladly publish them, and will fully indorse their efficacy. I
am confident that the reader will do well to preserve the receipts,
as, where they have been properly applied, I have never, in one
instance, known them to fail.

In the spelling of the Indian names I use a system of my own.
which is to spell words according to their sound in pronouncin
them. My translations may be thoroughly relied upon as being
accurate.

FROSTED MEMBERS.—The Indians make a plaster of the resin
of sap-pine, which has a soothing effect, and removes all irrita-
tion.

CHOLERA MORBUS.—Make a gruel of Was-lo-nee (rice) and a tea
of Han-to-la (liquorice). Then get a small quantity of Nee-ohar-lo
(red raspberry leaves), and make a strong tea, which must be given
to patient half a glassful every hour, or oftener, according to severity
of the case.

The red raspberry leaves are excellent in stopping looseness
of the bowels but care should be taken not to stop the looseness
suddenly.

RHEUMATISM.—This complaint is very prevalent among the Indians. Take equal parts of Alo-pinus (white pine bark), Lappee (burdock seeds), Alo-ja-ka (prickly-ash bark), and Nee-was-char (what is known as *Serpentaria Virginiana*, or Virginia snake root). Make a strong infusion, and drink freely through the day. The Indians while doctoring rheumatism make a free use of cold water applied to the parts afflicted, and give the patient a severe rubbing two or three times a day.

HOARSENESS, ASTHMA, COMPLAINTS OF THE BREAST, LUNGS, ETC.—Take of the leaves of hoarhound, dried, 2 ounces; infuse them for twenty-four hours in half a pint of boiling water (and I advise the addition of half a pint of spirits); strain, and add quarter of a pound of honey, and one teaspoonful of the essence of lemon.

Dose.—For adult one or two tablespoonfuls every two hours.

PULMONARY DISEASES.—(Especially efficacious for bleeding at the lungs.) Ne-bra-ta-hea (liverwort), ½ pound; Sa-bas-sa (Solomon's seal), ½ pound; Kee-chi-hee (skunk cabbage), ½ pound; Shu-jee (blood-root), 2 ounces; Pin-nee-se-ah (water hoarhound), ½ pound. Add a sufficient quantity of water; boil, and pour off the water till the strength is obtained; strain, and boil say to six porter bottlefuls, and add five pounds of strained honey; remove from the fire; (I then advise the addition of half a pint of brandy;) let it settle, and bottle for use. *Dose.*—A wine glassful three or four times a day.

N. B.—The Indians, by a preparation known only to themselves, make a liquid which forms an ingredient in nearly all their medicines. It takes the place of brandy and spirits, and therefore I advise the use of those liquids in several of the receipts given.

A VALUABLE POWDER.—Take equal parts of Wee-ne oh (pulverized mandrake); See-tu-bar (pulverized spearmint); Wano-to-o (cream of tartar). Mix. *Dose.*—A teaspoonful in tea or syrup.

The above receipt is useful in dieases of the liver, dyspepsia, obstructed menses, dropsy, in venereal diseases, and in every taint of the system.

CATARRH. (Snuff powder.)—Hon-kos-ka (high laurel), 1 ounce; Sa-wah-ja (sassafras), 1 ounce; Shu-jee (blood-root), 1 ounce. Pulverize; mix well.

INDIAN POULTICE.—Scrape the common carrot, add to it a decoction of Ag-ga-ga (spikenard root), and stir in Indian meal. They use the above poultice in case of inflammation bordering on gangrene or mortification.

TONIC TINCTURE.—Take of good sour or hard cider, 1 gallon, Aokee (white-oak bark), 2½ ounces; Whal-lo-ke (horseradish root), 4 ounces; Senecka-oko (Seneca snake root), 1½ ounce; carbonate of iron, 1½ ounce; Boel-lo-kee (golden seal root), 1 ounce; Mael-to-ha-nee (capsicum), ¼ ounce. Use.—A sure remedy for intermittent fevers, debility, and impoverished state of the blood. It is also excellent in obstructed menses, and the dropsy, worms, etc.

TINCTURE OF STRAMONIUM.—Pulverized seeds of Stramonium, 2 ounces; proof spirits, 1 quart. Let it stand one week. Dose.—Twenty-five drops twice a day. Use.—Cure of epilepsy, neuralgia, palpitation of the heart, and fits. The proof spirits act the same as the Indian ingredient—"Va-va-so-lee."

A VALUABLE VEGETABLE CAUSTIC.—Make a strong ley of hickory or oak ashes, put it into an iron kettle, and evaporate till dry; pulverize, and preserve it in closed vessels. The Indians use this caustic with great success. It is highly useful in the treatment of fistulas, also in indolent ulcers of every kind. It removes fungous flesh without exciting any inflammation, and acts but little, except on spongy or soft flesh. It is useful in cancers, and in every case where a caustic is required.

EXCELLENT EYEWATER.—Take of Sa-wah-ja (pith of sassafras), 1 drachm. Add to it a suitable quantity of rose-water. It will be found beneficial in the treatment of ophthalmia, or inflammation of the eyes

GARGLE.—Take Sa-moon (sage), 1 ounce; Rave-o-ee (hyssop), 1 ounce; pour on one quart of boiling water, and let it stand half an hour, then strain, and add 1 drachm of fine borax. *Use.*— This gargle is usefully employed by the Sioux tribe in aphthæ, and in quinsy or sore throat, particularly where there is acute inflammation.

GARGLE FOR PUTRID SORE THROAT.—Gee-sumach (bark of upland sumach); Lee-lo-we-nce (high blackberry); Alo-as-ter (common white elm bark); Alo-o-e-oh (white oak bark); Was-char-ee (small black snake-root); Sum-me, ah-ah (nanny berry bark). Take of each a handful, except the snake-root, which must be only half the quantity; make a strong decoction, add a piece of alum, and sweeten well with honey, then bottle for use. Apply often to the sores with a rag. It may at first irritate a little, but then cures. I have seen hundreds cured by this gargle where all other means were of no avail. In place of alum the Indians use a peculiar kind of grass, but the alum I know to be an excellent substitute from experience.

INFUSIONS.—Infusions, or, as they are usually called, *teas*, are a very common and good method used by the Indians, of administering the virtues of various medical agents. A two-fold benefit is derived from infusions: 1st, the medicinal properties of the article made use of; 2dly, the heat and diluent properties of the water.

During the year of my return (1872), which will be long remembered as one of epidemics, and general sickness, my success among my friends and acquaintances, in the treatment of various diseases, was so great that I was frequently urged by them to practise medicine professionally; and by the use of herb teas this success was accomplished.

An excellent method to make teas or infusions is to put the plant or root into a tea-pot, pour on boiling water, and let it stand a short time *by the side of the fire.* In this way the infusion is readily made very clear. For infusions generally, put a handful of the herb into a tea-pot, and add a quart of boiling water; when cool, drink freely.

For kidney complaint an excellent tea can be made of Tat-ta-lee (fleabane).

For weak lungs, coughs, pain in the breast, loss of appetite, dyspepsia, etc., the following tea will be found very beneficial.

Char-ee (snake-root); Boel-art (gold thread); Ga-no-ee-ah (centaury); Worlo-wanct (wormwood); Sy-an-zee (tansy); Dee-no-ee (boneset); Pin-nee-se-ah (hoarhound): of each one handful.

Dose.—To a large tablespoonful pour one pint of boiling water : when cold drink a wine glassful four times a day.

An excellent tea to expel worms is the following :

Ta-taa-ore (carolina pink), ½ an ounce; Ano-ano (senna), ¼ an ounce; Eno-ano (manna), ½ an ounce.

Dose.—Half a tea-cupful three or four times a day for a child six years old, or sufficient to purge.

The following tea, as a cleansing and cooling purgative, cannot be excelled. It is useful in fevers and inflammatory diseases.

Ano-ano (senna), ½ an ounce; Eno-ano (manna), ¼ an ounce; Sa-sa-poh (fennel seed, *bruised*), 1 teaspoonful.

Add to the above half an ounce of cream of tartar, after having put the senna and manna in one pint of boiling water, and strained it, then sweeten. In place of cream of tartar the Indians use a powder which they manufacture from laurel leaves, but as I do not know the formula, and do know the beneficial effect of cream of tartar, I advise the use of the latter.

Dose.—A wine glassful every hour till it purges.

The following preparation is used by the Indians in the treatment of *retention of urine*, etc. They use an ingredient called by them " Va-va-so-lee," but as that cannot be obtained, Holland gin will be found an excellent substitute.

Take of spearmint, green, *bruise*, and add sufficient quantity to saturate about one quart of Holland gin.

Dose.—The dose must be regulated according to the patient's habits. Some will require half, others a gill at a time, and repeated every thirty minutes. The patient should take it till it produces relief In cases where the *green* mint cannot be procured, the dry may be used, but it is not so good. This liquid may also be used beneficially, both externally and internally, in cases of severe vomiting

COMMON POULTICE.—Take of slippery elm bark (pulverized) a sufficient quantity; stir it in hot or warm milk and water, to the consistence of a poultice. This poultice exceeds every other in point of efficacy. It is of almost universal application, and removes inflammation sooner than any other. Compared to this, every other poultice dwindles into insignificance.

I will here add a bit of useful information not of Indian origin, but one of great benefit to suffering humanity. In scarlet fever, measles, whooping cough, and small pox (and all kindred diseases), give freely of brewer's yeast. Its effect is wonderful, the disease is forced out, and all fears of sore throat may be discarded where the yeast is given. In small pox, a regulation of the bowels, are of the yeast, and good, careful nursing (the room, in which the patient is placed, to be kept of an even temperature), will do more than all the doctors to be had. The patient's diet in this disease should consist chiefly of gruels, and warm teas should be frequently given. Take of saffron and catnip equal parts, make a tea, and give it warm. Use the fever remedies when fever appears.

Best nourishment for the disease is *barley water, Indian meal gruel, buttermilk and water, roasted apples, and ripe fruit* moderately.

Let there be a current of air in the room, but avoid the same coming in contact with the patient. Great attention must be paid to cleanliness. Change linen and clothes often. If eruptions are large, full of water and irritating, puncture same, and sprinkle same with dry flour of slippery elm, and the pitting of the face will be greatly diminished.

In conclusion allow me to assure the reader that all the foregoing receipts are of great value, and may be fully relied upon. When you go to the druggist be particular to write the exact quantity as given by me, and make use of the *English names*, only, as very few druggists have any knowledge of the Indian languages.

The Indians have great faith in the healing qualities of tobacco and I have seen many cures by its use, such as stings of bees, bites of insects, etc.

[We have seen several persons who have been cured by Miss Barber, and we have no hesitation in asserting that her Indian receipts are of great value. The lady previous to her life among the Indians was a great student, and principal among her studies was that of medicine.

THE PUBLISHERS.]